Urban Gothic

2

More of Tales of Pillage,
Debauchery, *and* Looting,
from the author
who brought you
Urban Gothic

By Jason Goodman

"Whoever tells the truth is chased out of nine villages."

— Turkish Proverb

"Craft may have clothes,
but truth loves to go naked."

— Thomas Fuller

Other Books by the Author:

BLOOD ON MY HANDS and a knife in my back
SIMPLE REFLECTIONS on a frozen surface
NERVOUS READER
NERVOUS READER second edition
a. PUZZLED EXISTENCE
Urban Gothic

Available at Amazon.com or wherever fine books are sold.

DISCLAIMER

During the research and writing of this book, every attempt was made to disguise the identities of the individuals portrayed. Names have been changed. Time periods and exact locations have been altered whenever reference is made to a particular individual or event.

However, the author wants to clarify that every story in this book is based on facts, diverging from the absolute truth only in the circumstances described above. The author considers the identity of the characters depicted in these stories to be "Everyman." Thus, *Urban Gothic 2* stands as a metaphor for the trials and tribulations of all of humanity.

Inquiries:

Alchemy Studio, Inc. Art & Design – Fine literary works
Lititz, Pennsylvania, and Westport, Ireland
www.alchemystudioinc.com

Front-cover design and back-cover photograph by:
Jason P. Goodman

Cover Design:
Joshua Riggan

Copy Editing/Proofreading:
Frank W. Kresen
www.artisanproofpositive.com
artisan :: *proof positive*
professional graphic design and editorial services

Interior Layout Design:
Kimberly A. Walsh
www.artisankimwalsh.com

Printed in the United States of America
ISBN#: # 978-0-692-14497-8
Library of Congress Control Number: 2017900181

Table of Contents

The Stories

Dedication

This volume is dedicated to the two women in my life who have had the most influence on it — my wife, Teresa, and my mother, Mary T. Goodman.

I owe you both for my life.

In 1970, I returned from Vietnam with a "frozen soul."

My wife, Teresa, helped me to defrost it and showed me what love is.

My mother, Mary T., filled my head with words and dreams.

Preface

It would be rather easy to tell you, the reader, that a prerequisite for getting everything out of this book that it has to offer is to read *Urban Gothic*, the first book in this series.

Naturally, that would reek of a sales pitch, like I was trying to get you to buy the first volume of short stories.

But, in all honesty, the reader can get everything out of this book without having to first read *Urban Gothic*.

Urban Gothic 2 stands alone as a volume of both enlightening and entertaining short stories. Every single one of these stories is based on an actual occurrence. These are all true stories, based on true facts and true circumstances. The only thing I have changed in the retelling is the names of the people involved. This was done for simple protection from legal abuse.

My entire life has been one continuous story. I started relating this fact with an autobiography, *a. PUZZLED EXISTENCE*, published in 2010.

That book covers 60 years of my life, from 1950 up to and including 2010. You could say that it's one, long, drawn-out story of existence.

But the *Urban Gothic* series stories are the fill-ins. These short stories introduce the humanity into that 60-year struggle. More importantly, they provide the most important element — laughter.

Unless your pulse rate is around 10, I can almost guarantee you that you will find most of these stories humorous. As *Homo Sapiens* — life's idiot species — we come into this world completely helpless. We can't get up and run just a few minutes after we are born. We can't crawl to our mother's breast under our own power for nourishment — it must be provided. Our needs are manifold during those early, formative years. Rather than a liability, I see this as a cause for celebration and study. What we lack in those early years is made up for a hundred-fold later on when we become fully grown human beings.

And that is where the humor should introduce itself. We were helpless — having survived that, we should all laugh our heads off. Many television programs of the "hidden camera" variety have capitalized on portraying and exposing human foibles — outlandish stupidity, mankind caught in the act of being just that — human.

I would not go so far as to say that these are "human-interest" stories, but, then again, maybe one of my critics will do just that. What I do know for a fact is this: I have experienced every one of the stories that this book comprises. I have lived through their inception and through most of their outcomes. Some of these tales just can't be made up. It would be impossible to weave a seamless thread of made-up factoids and have them come out as true, humorous short stories.

Again, allow me to suggest that you consider looking into the original *Urban Gothic* after reading this volume. I strongly believe that taking that simple action will provide a panorama of human interaction.

Introduction

I was both surprised and elated when Jason Goodman asked me to write the introduction to his second volume of short stories, *URBAN GOTHIC 2*. What follows, therefore, is a mini-story of our short but very special friendship.

Jason and I met one day while working out in a small-town gym in Lititz, Pennsylvania. That led to our becoming fast friends. In some ways, we were an unlikely match. I was age 85, Jason 68. I am a retired Protestant minister; Jason is an avowed agnostic. He experienced a tough mountainside upbringing in the coal region of Northeastern Pennsylvania. I was born and reared on the Philadelphia Main Line and was reared in a Protestant historic peace church. By age eighteen, Jason had enlisted in the U.S. Navy and was on his way to Vietnam, while at eighteen I had begun my college pre-medical studies, which exempted me from the Korean War. Nevertheless, Jason and I found much in common. We shared German heritage, hard-working fathers, artistic mothers, intellectual inquiry, progressive thinking, a love of literature and the arts, travel, honesty, morality, dependability, and advocacy for peace with justice.

The two different pathways taken in our late teens led to eventual outcomes unanticipated by either of us. Jason developed a broad range of skills and experience. He's a disciplined workhorse who can operate bulldozers, build houses, repair trucks, and restore automobiles. He's a designer, innovator, and accomplished artist. He's a published writer, poet, and regular editorial contributor to our local town newspaper. Jason tackles the day's most divisive issues, boldly and fearlessly speaking out on economic, political, educational, and religious controversies. Jason forces people to think, to defend what they believe and preach. Yet, best of all, this guy is a warmhearted, faithful friend, who has that rare gift of humor, the innate ability to make people laugh.

Jason is a survivor. Having returned from Vietnam physically impaired and severely traumatized from shrapnel wounds, Agent Orange damage, alcohol addiction, and psychological trauma, my good friend has spent years in post-surgical recoveries, living with unremitting pain, faithfully attending AA meetings, and undergoing psychotherapeutic counseling for PTSD.

Jason's unique gifts as a renowned artist, writer, and storyteller provide the best healing and wellness therapy of all. Two of his acrylic paintings hang on the walls of my home. Whenever I pause before these unique iridescent acrylic canvases, something deep within me feels pure joy! My friends often experience something similar when they view these compositions. Jason's work evokes understanding coupled with a peculiar satisfaction. This experience I have found in his writing as well.

Jason's gift of writing grabs one's attention, also. Read *a. PUZZLED EXISTENCE*, his hair-raising autobiography, and you will better understand the full range of this special individual. You may also enjoy editions one or two of *Nervous Reader*, poetry by Jason Goodman. But I am writing today to introduce you to Jason's latest collection of humorous short stories.

URBAN GOTHIC 2, like *URBAN GOTHIC*, is intended to bring you many laughs. As I said earlier, Jason has lived in many parts of the U.S. — and other countries as well —working, studying, teaching, instructing, painting, writing, and having all kinds of unimaginable fun. His *URBAN GOTHIC* stories are funny, half crazy, perhaps a bit raw or shocking in parts for some folk, yet interesting, amusing, provocative, life embracing, and, according to Jason, absolutely true!

So — good therapy for the writer and for us, his readers? Absolutely.

The special friendship that Jason and I have enjoyed has led us to push each other (hard) in our daily gym workouts, enjoy stimulating conversations over coffee, give encouragement to one another during tough times or days of pain, and then occasionally "*...break bread with our wives,*" to use my friend's endearing words.

We agree on this one thing: for whatever reason, we were meant to meet. Whether this is God's doing, or fate, or some mystically inexplicable happening, I will be forever grateful.

Now, please sit down and have fun with *URBAN GOTHIC 2*. Enjoy this guy's short stories, and allow yourself some good laughs.

W. Clemens Rosenberger, DDiv

The Stories

Louie's Pooch and the Two Pure-White Wedding Albums

In a previous book of mine, *Urban Gothic,* I talked about my friend Louie. There were a few stories revolving around him because we were partners in a thriving LSD business and just good friends in general.

Well, Louie married this young lady and settled down — as much as a person like Louie could settle down, I suppose. But I was in town and gave him a call, proposing that we get together. At that time, he and his wife were renting an apartment in one of those swinging singles' complexes that rental companies situate in wooded surroundings. So I went up to their place to enjoy an afternoon of chitchat and finger foods.

On that occasion, it was summertime, and we were all in the living room, drinking gin and tonics. Because I had been out of the country, I hadn't been able to attend their gala wedding. Louie's bride, beaming with pride, brought out her two pure-white wedding albums.

Now, I don't like looking at pictures, anyway. In fact, nowadays, people just hand you their phones to show you photos. But I wanted to be congenial, so I sat there and waded through all the smiling faces in their wedding garb.

What happened next is the crux of this little story.

Louie's wife, Ruth, left the books on the coffee table in the living room, and we adjourned to the deck to enjoy the sunshine — a rare commodity in this Wyoming valley. We also enjoyed a continuous supply of gin and tonic — copious amounts of gin and tonic.

Ruth went into the apartment to refresh our drinks, and we heard an ear-shattering scream.

Louie and Ruth always had Dachshunds — in fact, they were breeders of that type of dog. At the time, they had four of those little sausage hounds, but they weren't the problem. It was the other dog. Louie had picked up this ugly, scruffy, mixed-breed dog that had the personality of a wolverine. I forget what he called this animal, but it was one of those "rescue" dogs — before the term was ever coined. In the mid-1970s, a dog like that would not have been "rescued" from anything except a well-placed shot behind the ear.

Hearing the aforementioned scream, Louie and I went running up to the sliding glass doors and found Ruth sitting in the middle of the living-room floor, just wailing, with tears streaming down her face. The mutt had gotten into both of those pure-white wedding albums, which were scattered all over the living room. I had never seen a dog do so much damage in such a short period of time. There wasn't a piece of those photos that was more than two inches square. The dog had ripped them to shreds.

At that point, I decided that *The Afternoon of the Never-Ending Gin and Tonics* was over, and I quietly walked through and let myself out via the front door.

Because I was living elsewhere at the time, I never had an opportunity to speak to Louie about this brazen act on the part of a dog that he had rescued from sure death.

Many years later, Louie heard that I was in town and called to invite me to dinner at their "new" house, and I accepted.

The three of us sat at their small, square dining-room table, eating a very nice dinner, as Ruth was an excellent cook. Six Dachshunds were running around at our feet under the table, barking up a storm. It was such a loud

cacophony of noise that, at first, I thought
that Louie and Ruth had both gone deaf. I
soon realized that they were simply tuning out
this bark-storm because they had grown so
accustomed to it.

While all of this was going on, that same
scruffy mutt came hobbling out. This guy was
old — he had gray hair and whiskers and
walked like an old man. He came out from
behind the couch and made an attempt at
barking but soon broke into a fit of doggie
coughing.

I said, "Louie — you still have that little
bastard?"

Louie went on to relate the story of how, after
the incident involving the pure-white wedding
albums, he'd gone and got his gun. He was
going to blow this dog into next week. But he
underwent a change of heart, relenting at the
last minute, and he resolved to do everything in
his power to keep the thing alive.

And that is what he did. He treated that dog
like crap but attended to his every medical
need — at great expense, I might add — just to
make the animal suffer for as long as possible.
And, at that, Louie had succeeded. The dog was
more than 15 years old and had the personality
to match — that of a bitter old man.

Louie told me that they absolutely hated each other. He said that once, he had fallen asleep on the couch and that this little assassin had snuck up and bit him on the dick. For a second time, Louie fetched his *pistola*, intending to blow this dog away. Instead, he just bandaged up his cock and kept the dog alive for several more years.

It was an interesting story. I never thought that my friend Louie was that devious — instead of simply ending this dog's life, he went the other way, down a path of pure cruelty.

Eventually the dog died of extremely old age — and they never did replace the two pure-white wedding albums.

Sourdough Suicide

*W*e rented a house that was located about 200 yards from the beach in Boynton Beach, Florida. I was with my second wife at the time, and this eventually became the house that Jack built — well, no; it was the place where my marriage to this woman came to an end.

But that's another story entirely.

The place was small but very quaint — although I'm not sure that word is applicable in south Florida. I know it's a word often used on the northeast US coast, in places like Boston, Salem, or even Peyton Place. Yes — that's the ticket: it's *sooooo* "quaint" here.

I'm getting carried away, so I'd better chart a new course if we are going to get anywhere with this story.

The little house had one bedroom, a living room of sorts, and a small kitchen. It was comfortable. Well, it *must* have been, because we spent more than five years there.

My Number 2 (Doesn't that sound like an old British war movie? As in, "Why, yes, Briggs. This is my Number 2 here. Yes, a very capable man, I must say….")

But back to the page.

My Number 2 had a habit of wrapping everything in tin foil. I mean, *everything*. One day, I pulled this tiny, little package out of the refrigerator and unwrapped it. The thing contained two — I repeat, *two* — green stuffed olives. Some days, the inside of our fridge looked like a damned bauxite mine.

My Number 2 used to travel up to Indiana for the Christmas holidays. I made the trip once and swore never to make that mistake again. Her parents had a small house, so they would set up a folding bed at night for me in the living room, right next to the Christmas tree. When I woke up in the morning, I'd be staring at my father-in-law's feet. His recliner opened up right to the head of the folding bed.

Also, the damn liquor stores in Indiana would close at some ungodly early hour. I went through a New Year's Eve with one can of Iron City Beer and a small glass of *crème de menthe*. So, I said "No more" after that first trip.

So, there I was one Christmas season, sexually frustrated and living alone near the beach in south Florida. It was great! One day, a brand-new convertible pulled down the alley next to my house. Out stepped Joe and Tom, two old friends of mine who had some really bad habits. They opened the trunk of the car to reveal a case of assorted booze and mixers. Then Tom waved a plastic bag in front of me that was chock full of a white substance that, when inhaled, makes a man's dick shrivel up. Tom and Joe were looking for fun.

There we were, three *compadres*, all away from their wives, with plenty of money, booze, and nose candy — the perfect recipe for attracting a sexually transmitted disease in south Florida. They told me to throw some clothes in a bag, grab some cash, and get in the car — we were heading south, to the Florida Keys!

Before I left, there was one responsibility I had to take care of. My wife had told me to "feed her sourdough."

She had this big glass jar in the fridge that was full of sourdough starter. I really didn't pay much attention to it, because she rarely baked anything. I think she kept it only because she'd been in San Francisco once and a friend had given it to her. The friend told her that this particular sourdough went back to the first human beings who walked upright. It would have been a lot easier if her friend had just given her one of those cheap plastic souvenir replicas of Coit Towers or the Fulton Fish Market. But, *noooooo* — it had to be sourdough.

In fact, I think that my Number 2 and her San Francisco friend had had a giant piss-up and weren't speaking to each other — which was even more reason to 86 the sourdough, because you had to "feed" it.

I swear, it wasn't like you had to clean its cage, but you did have to feed this stuff. It lived on flour and sugar. Before my wife left for Indiana, she'd had me repeat, word for word, the process and the portion calculations of the feeding process. Naturally, I only half listened, because I didn't like this stuff in my reefer to begin with. But I smiled and parroted back the words. With Joe and Tom outside revving the engine and tapping the horn, I was in a hurry. My penis was already pointing south, and my gonads were lying on the beach at Big Pine Key.

I couldn't remember the exact formula, so I just dumped in a bag each of flour and sugar, threw in some water, and headed out the door.

We went down to the Keys and had one of those memorable times that you can never quite remember clearly due to the ingestion of copious amounts of liquor and other nefarious substances that are all on the evening news these days. We all succeeded in getting laid, which isn't that big of an accomplishment in south Florida if you have a pulse and some money (a few of your natural teeth are always nice but not really necessary).

After about a week, we returned to my little house in Boynton Beach. They pulled up, shoved me out of the car, and proceeded to drive to Palm Beach International Airport to catch their flight.

I staggered into the house, hung over and suffering from sleep deprivation, and decided to sleep for a week or two. But before I started that, a nice, cold drink was definitely on the agenda. I walked up to the refrigerator, pulled open the door, and out plopped this huge blob — right onto my bare feet (I'd lost my shoes somewhere in the Keys).

It was this big, pulsating blob of dough. Bubbles would erupt, like the mud pots in Yellowstone Park — *Bloop! Bloop!* This thing was gross. I spent the next three days cleaning up this mess. The blob had grown large enough to block the cold-air fan or something, and that had allowed the temperature inside the fridge to rise indefinitely. That, together with the way-too-much "food" that I'd fed it, allowed this thing to assume grandiose proportions.

It was a complete mess. I had to practically chisel this stuff off of the metal shelves and use a putty knife on the inside walls. Finally, after hours of backbreaking work, I'd restored the fridge to its original condition.

Unfortunately, the sourdough didn't make it. I held a formal wake, and everyone paid their respects and left condolences — except one person. When my *La Numera Dos* came home, she went straight for the refrigerator. I heard a loud scream, followed by "Where's my sourdough!?"

That was when I had to break the news to her. It wasn't something that I took pleasure in, but someone had to do it. I was the one who had to tell her that the sourdough had committed suicide. It turned out to be grounds for divorce.

That stupid sourdough cost me a small fortune.

NyQuil Debacle

*I*t was a cold night, and I was sitting in my studio with the old potbelly coal stove blazing full blast. It wasn't a good time for me, having just flown in from Florida in that rarified air that only airline cabins can create. To be quite honest, I felt like crap. A cold had freely been given to me by one of those fellow travelers, and, naturally, I accepted it. Hell — the thing was free for the taking.

On the way to my place, I'd stopped and purchased a bottle of "NyQuil." You know the stuff — a thick, gooey syrup that is supposed to vanquish your cold in a matter of hours. So, I started sipping on this stuff, waiting for this elixir to kick in.

In the back of my mind, a thought took root: Why not pop down to Vispi's and have a cocktail? No one knew that I was in town, so the chances of Barbara finding me were quite slim. Vispi's was an elegant cocktail lounge located in Edwardsville, Pennsylvania. Joe Vispi was gay, although he was also married and had a daughter. Go figure. But, over the years, I'd managed to score in Vispi's on a regular basis, due to the fact that there weren't too many straight guys in the place.

Now, I was sick as a dog, and my better judgment was screaming at me to just stay in, but did I listen?

Nooooooo.

I had an appendage with a brainless head. He hung around with two nuts and lived next door to an asshole; he was telling me it was *imperative* that I go out. Everything was wrong: It was cold and miserable out, and I was really sick, but that damned "NyQuil" was providing a *faux* sense of security. It was starting to roll around in my bloodstream, conspiring against me: *Yeah — it's OK to go out. You don't feel that bad. And, after a few pops, you'll feel even better….*

Better judgment be damned. I re-dressed and went down to Vispi's. But, contrary to what my mind was telling me, I didn't feel any better. By this time, I'd ingested the entire bottle of "NyQuil," and it didn't seem like it was helping one bit.

So, I sat there nursing one drink. It was a Manhattan, if my memory serves me correctly. My old-time bartender Leo was behind "the plank," but he was not the kind of guy to make small talk. This was an interesting fact about Vispi's. There were all of these gay guys swishing around — and then there was Leo. Leo had one of those "You call yourself a Marine?" buzz-cuts. He was fairly well built and had the temperament of a crosstown bus driver. I mean, Leo wasn't disrespectful — he just never made small talk, or chitchat, that sort of stuff.

Anyway, I just sat there wallowing in my misery, sipping on this drink, which, combined with the gooey sweetness of that damned "NyQuil" crap, just wasn't making it. Also, another mitigating fact was the forecast for bad weather. It was supposed to snow like hell, and no one wanted to go out.

This was another thing. I lived in Florida — the Palm Beach area, to be exact — and everyone knows that the weather is decidedly better in Florida than in Wilkes-Barre, Pennsylvania. I would travel up there about three times a year, usually for the holidays, and I hated every minute of it. I don't know if you realize it, but Wilkes-Barre is a real dump.

The place is depressing as hell. So, that —
combined with lousy weather — would make
anyone order another Manhattan.

My second drink was a waste of resources.
Instead of getting better, I was feeling worse.
After about 15 minutes into *Cocktail Numero
Dos,* I made the fateful decision to pack it up
and return to my studio.

At the time, I was driving a little 1967
Mustang coupe. It was a nice car that I'd bought
off my old man earlier in the day. The plan was
to drive it back to Florida when my break was
over.

There I was, driving up Main Street in the
armpit called Edwardsville, Pennsylvania,
gripping the steering wheel with both hands
and trying to coax some heat out of the
dashboard. I don't know how fast I was driving
— didn't have a clue, really.

But then I came up to the area in front of Vic
Mars Restaurant.

There were two seafood restaurants in
Edwardsville — Vic Mars and Konafolds. I
never liked Vic Mars. They said that he used
to disguise bad seafood, and then, one year, he
was busted for watering down his liquor. But
some people swore by the joint. Personally, I
preferred Konafolds. My buddy Carl and I used

to go there to eat clams and drink beer. Do you remember that? Drinking the little cup of liquid butter after all the clams were gone, and then chomping down on a fresh saltine cracker. Good stuff.

Anyway, back to Vic Mars. As I came up to the area, a second set of headlights appeared in my windshield. There was one car stopped in front of Vic Mars and another coming down the hill. At the last moment, it started swinging into my lane. So I jerked the steering wheel in a hard right, and that's when the fun began.

They said that I wrecked seven cars that night — six parked on the street and, of course, mine. My Mustang ended up in the back of a station wagon. I had somehow managed to rip both front fenders off my car, and then I ran up into this other car.

The police officer who arrested me turned out to be my friend Carl. Now, Carl was fully aware that, at any given moment, I had at least three different valid driver's licenses, so he asked me for the cleanest one. After a few hours in the lockup, I was driven back to my studio by Carl. During the ride back, I explained that I'd had only one drink. That much was true. But I'd drunk an entire bottle of that damned "NyQuil," and that's what pushed me over the legal limit for blood alcohol content.

But this isn't what I wanted to tell you about.

Sure, I wrecked a bunch of cars and received a DUI for my troubles. They took my license, and, after six months, it was mailed back to me. But what happened next is the real gist of my story.

At that time, I had insured this Mustang with Liberty Mutual Insurance Company. They took care of everything, and we all moved on.

At the time of the aforementioned accident, Liberty Mutual operated in Pennsylvania only. Well, several years later, I needed insurance for another automobile, and I had been living out of state for years. Here I was, back in Pennsylvania, needing insurance, so I called Liberty Mutual. The girl on the phone asked me my name and then asked me to spell my last name. *No problemo.* "It's G-O-O-D-M-A-N." She was quiet for a minute or two, and then she started laughing like crazy.

I asked, "What's so funny?"

She told me that I had a lot of nerve calling them for automobile insurance after that debacle in Edwardsville, Pennsylvania. I assumed that they were still making payments on the damage I had caused.

The funny thing is that I'd forgotten all about that little accident in front of Vic Mars Seafood Restaurant — the night that I was busted for drinking that damned "NyQuil."

Neanderthal Orange

*T*hings were tough at Florida Atlantic University. I would do just about anything to make a buck. The art department was looking for nude models for their life-drawing classes. At $10 an hour, it was a no-brainer. I was just the man for the job. Back in the mid-'70s, $10 an hour was a lot of money. Plus, because I was an up-and-coming art instructor, I would need to know about these things. I figured that the experience would serve me well later on, when I was the one teaching the life-drawing class.

The university had its own newspaper, *The Atlantic Owl,* named after the burrowing owl, which lived off campus throughout the abandoned World War II airfields, where many universities had been built. No, I'm not making this stuff up. With a service like Google, it is difficult to spin a tall tale anymore.

I became a freelance reporter for the newspaper; they paid me $30 an article. I would write articles that were of some public-service value to the students. One of these dealt with the proliferation of 99-cent breakfast places scattered around Boca Raton. It was true — you could get coffee, toast, and hashbrowns, not to mention the three-eggs-any-style. It was a good deal, so I went about, checking out the many different offerings. Some of the joints were really "choke and puke" places. It was my job to inform the students which ones to avoid entirely.

I also served as an "RA" — a Resident Assistant. I was paid $60 a month, given a private room, usually right next to the steps, a telephone in my room, and a few other benefits. The job consisted of checking students into and out of the dormitories — well, the dorm that I was attached to, anyway.

Simultaneously, I worked for the university in their maintenance department. The job — usually a 20-hour work week — paid $4 an hour, and I did whatever the regular guys didn't want to do — mostly a lot of shit work. But I didn't care. That extra money put me over the top in terms of weekly income. You may laugh at all these random, unconnected forms of employment, but I look at it this way: When I finished college, I didn't owe anyone a cent!

One of the last things that I did to earn extra money was to establish a winery on campus. That's absolutely correct — I made wine in my RA dorm room. It was, after all, a "private" room. I made wine and sold it for $2 a bottle. This stuff was really rotgut, if you want to know the truth. I never drank the stuff myself, but I did manage to attract a slew of regular customers — why, I'll never know. It had nothing to do with the taste — I can assure you of that. Some of these guys wouldn't wait for the damn stuff to ferment. They would stop by almost every day, asking if it was ready. I forget the exact time frame, but I think this fine vintage required at least three weeks.

Here's what I did: First, you have to find four glass gallon-jugs, the type that apple juice used to come in. Then you had to find some really big balloons, the kind that can float a weather station into orbit. You'd place real fruit juice into the jug, followed by yeast that came in block form, and then add copious amounts of sugar. Then you'd fill it with warm water and place the balloon over the mouth of the jug, secure it really tightly with a rubber band, and then just sit back and wait. As the wine fermented, the balloon would blow up — up to 18 inches in diameter (that's why it had to be one of those really big jobs). Then the balloon would start slowly to deflate; when it had returned to its normal size, the wine was ready.

The secret was not to have any preservatives in the juice. It could be from concentrate, but it had to be free of chemicals. I would make grape, apple, and finally, orange wine.

At this point, I would love to give you the exact formula for the wine, but I'm not going to. This isn't out of any love for mankind or concern for the health of the next generation. It's a lot simpler than that. I have just forgotten — that's all.

I used a piece of plastic tubing to decant the mixture into whatever wine bottles I could find. Hell, sometimes, I just used soda bottles. Each gallon jug would produce about 3 fifths of wine. This was truly the nectar of the gods — the only question was: Which god? I wouldn't tell anyone that my wine was the favorite of Pluto, the Roman god that ruled over Hades!

I gave each vintage a name. There was *Awful Apple, Gangrene Grape,* and the best one (my favorite) was *Neanderthal Orange.*

The third floor of this particular dorm was entirely occupied by Cuban students. Each month, they would throw a party. They had a sandwich-board sign that said, simply,

"Tsunami Tonight!" This is what they called their parties, and trust me, they were definitely parties that washed away everything in their path! These Cuban boys really knew how to throw a party! Besides the usual kegs of beer, they would send an envoy down to my second-floor room and order *Neanderthal Orange* wine. They literally loved this stuff, something that never failed to amaze me, because it was really obnoxious. But every drop of that wine that I could produce went to their Tsunami parties.

After I graduated with my second bachelor's degree, I sold my "winery" to some fool, complete with my secret recipes. Whether or not the Cubans kept up their trade with him, I'll never know. But I gather that the tradition of fine wines emanating from the campus of FAU in Boca Raton, Florida, lived on — fine vintages for the masses.

Mother's Lunch

*M*ary T. Goodman was definitely *not* Mrs. June Cleaver or Martha Stewart.

My mother came from the New York City area and was quite an accomplished woman before she even met my Dad. Mary T. studied art at the Fawcett School. She was a draftsperson, and she'd helped design the folding wing of the Hellcat aircraft used during the Second World War. She attended MIT as the first female student and didn't marry until she was well into her late twenties — something that was unheard of back in the 1920s. She drove a roadster with a rumble seat and belonged to the Polar Bear Club, a group that swam in the Atlantic Ocean in mid-January. You would be right in thinking that she was not inclined to be very domestic.

There were five of "us" — my dad, me, and my three brothers. Early in the morning, Mary T. would be out there in the kitchen, preparing brown-bag lunches for the whole lot. She would throw out the slices of "Fluff" bread like some Las Vegas card shark, and they would land as if she were playing a game of White-Bread Solitaire.

She would then bring out the various condiments — peanut butter, lunchmeat (usually bologna, also known as "Football Meat"), plus any leftover bacon from breakfast (which rarely happened), and whatever else she had floating around inside the icebox.

Mary T. also had out the mustard, pickles, and other "toppings" to go with the various by-products that sandwiches are made up of.

At the beginning of the school year, we used to settle into a routine of trading lunches. Some kids' moms really went to town with their lunchboxes, placing all kinds of goodies in there. Fat chance of that ever happening to me — I'll tell you that right upfront. The nuns would take all of our lunches and place them on the windowsill, right above the giant, cast-iron steam radiators, so the interior of the lunch bag got really good and hot. This wasn't a bad thing if you had a simple cheese sandwich; it would be melted by lunchtime. The thing that really bothered me was that they would put the chocolate milk and cheap orange drink up there, also. I hated the hot-milk treatment.

Well, after about a week, my friends would run away screaming if I offered to trade my lunch with them. They would swear never to make that mistake again. I'll tell you how this terrible chain of events came about, depriving me of those well-made school lunches that Beaver Cleaver would tote to school.

You see, my mother wasn't your typical housewife. In fact, she hated that title and everything it stood for. She was president of the local chapter of the League of Women Voters, president of the local Business and Professional Women's Club, and a member of the Republican party, with all of the trappings that entailed. She was probably the *only* Republican in that entire god-forsaken place called Wilkes-Barre. So, you can guess that making lunches was not very high up on her social calendar.

When she married my old man and they moved from Baltimore to the dirty, depressing, and disgusting environs of Wyoming Valley, a thriving coal-mining town at that time, it must have been like leaving Earth and colonizing Mars. Hell, she went from the jazz clubs of Manhattan to an outhouse and a well that you had to defrost to get water out of. She left central heat and ended up with coal stoves and a fireplace in the dead of winter.

Of course, all of this misery was shared with her four indentured servants, her sons.

Getting back to the lunchbox trilogy: She could slather on mustard and peanut butter with complete abandon. Mayo and catsup would be plopped on various pieces of breads, not to mention the serious ingredients. Those, of course, were the meats, bananas, and that disgusting stuff that came in a little can, Deviled Ham. It was definitely something that Satan would have enjoyed, as far as I was concerned. There was always some Spam to go into the mix, too.

But here is where the entire thing came undone. Even with all the best intentions, Mary T. would just start flipping two halves of sandwiches together. But she wasn't ever paying attention. Why should she? It wasn't she who had to eat this gruel.

The consequences of her inattention were what you might call Hybrid Sandwiches. To me, they were more like mutations. You could end up with peanut butter and mustard, or bananas on top of Deviled Ham. The combinations were limitless. Whatever nightmare between two slices of bread your depraved imagination could conceive of became a reality in the hands of my mother.

Now you understand why my friends would go running off in sheer terror at the prospect of sharing or trading a lunch. But even that wasn't the worst-case scenario. The really grand stuff of nightmares was grabbing my dad's lunch by mistake. For some odd reason, his selection was even more grotesque. His sandwiches were particularly more obscene, resembling some type of black-arts worship in their construction. I used to imagine that their formulas came from some old Greek text, a book that had been banned by the Church thousands of years prior. His between-the-slices would be pickles and strawberry jelly, or Spam and bananas. Try some delicious bologna and chocolate sauce — that was an all-time favorite.

Now you understand why I am afflicted with several conditions of the mind in my adult life. Just the thought of Mary T.'s sandwiches — just writing about them, right here on this page — has set back my therapy by a decade. Tonight, I will not sleep. I will taste chocolate sauce and Spam all night. The lights will have to stay on just to guarantee that there aren't any of these demon sandwiches lurking in my bedroom.

The Art Work

*H*ave you ever noticed that some people have weird first names?

By that, I mean they seem to live in their names. Let me explain.

Throughout my life, everyone I knew who was named "George" *had* to be named "George." A "George" type is always just that — a person named "George."

I know this sounds ridiculous, but bear with me.

"George" people are always a little bit strange. Granted, we can all be strange at times, but, for some reason, people named "George" are always a little more strange than usual. Every "George" I have ever known has had some weird quirks about him.

There was this one "George" who was so anal retentive, I felt that he should consider taking medication. He invited me into his basement one day, and it was a trip. Every screw was named and marked. There were all of these little baby-food jars hanging on the wall. Each one had certain-sized screws in it, and they all had labels stating what type and size screw they held.

But it didn't stop there.

He had all of his tools meticulously outlined on the wall in white paint. He could tell at a glance when something went missing. I had this incredible urge to mess things up a bit — like change a few jars around so that the label didn't match the screw.

Hell, George's entire basement looked like that — everything had its place, and it was all labeled. It wasn't like the public was invited down into this monument to efficiency. That would have kept George up all night — just the thought of strangers roaming around in his basement, touching things, moving things around. If something like that would happen, George would have had to be restrained.

Well, I knew this other guy named "George." He was from a little town called Courtdale. Now, you must understand that Courtdale itself was a strange little town. It had a history of sorts. Plus, it had Hoppy's Bar, and that, in itself, is saying quite a bit.

Courtdale was this little place that waited

years to get hooked up to the local sewer authority. They dug up the main street, the only street that runs through Courtdale, installed the giant sewer pipes, covered it all back up, and repaved the street.

The people of Courtdale, who were all named "George," decided to wait 10 years before they hooked their homes up to this brand-new invention. Just think: It would do away with their chamber pots.

Anyway, there are a lot of other reasons that Courtdale, Pennsylvania, is strange, but that isn't the gist of this story. George is the gist — the guy from Courtdale.

For some reason that I care not to recall, George needed a place to sleep. This was a strange request, because his parents' house, in — you guessed it — Courtdale, was less than two miles away, and he would have had to walk past at least six barrooms to get there.

Well, George asked me if he could stay in my studio for the night. This was my famous "Alchemy Studio," in Larksville, the less-weird town, just south of Courtdale. I opened this studio in 1970, right after returning from Vietnam, and used it off and on until 2006 — that's 36 years!

My place was inside an old coal-mine-office

building called "The Boston Coal Company."
It was a red-brick structure, built in 1868 (my
dad did the research on the place). So, you
know the place was definitely haunted. At least,
I knew it was haunted. (Again, that's another
story completely.)

So, crazy George asked me if he could use
my studio, which consisted of one large room
and a small room in the back. It was heated
with a potbelly stove — that was it, the only
heat source. The place didn't have a bathroom
until much, much later in its life. At the time
that George used it for that one night, you
had to go out back behind the building to do
your business. In the summertime, there were
grapevines that you could hide behind while
you relieved yourself, but this was in the dead
of winter.

I had a place to stay at the time. The house
of one of my girlfriends was made available to
me. Now that I think of it, George was probably
aware of this — he knew that I wasn't sleeping
in my studio at the time. But it was set up for
sleeping. In the corner was a rather comfortable
single bed with a nice quilt on it.

Another thing about this story is the fact that
George wasn't alone. He had a dog who went
everywhere with him.

The following morning, I drove up to my studio in Larksville to do some work and basically just check on the place — because George was strange, as I explained earlier. Well, when I opened the door, a great stench nearly knocked me off my feet. The place reeked with the smell of poop. I mean, *serious* poopy smells. So, with my handkerchief over my face, I entered the studio, and this is what I found.

In the middle of the room, right in front of a very cold potbelly stove, was a pizza box. This large-size pizza box had two — yes, *two* — piles of fecal matter in it, one from George and the other from the ass of his dog, Brutus.

Next to the pizza box was a little scrap of paper, and written on it were these words: "We left a sculpture for you as payment for our stay!" Signed, G E O R G E.

A Tale Told in Woe

*T*he Veterans Administration Hospital in Wilkes-Barre, Pennsylvania, is a really cool place to hang out.

With that statement, you would be correct in assuming that Wilkes-Barre isn't the most exciting place in the United States. The fact of the matter is that this town can be pretty disgusting.

One day I was in Wilkes-Barre, hanging out at the Veterans Hospital with a bunch of grumpy old warriors, waiting for the pharmacy to fill our prescriptions. These old farts were complaining about everything they could possibly think of. After a while, I grew tired of all this noise. So, I stood up and told them to go and buy very expensive healthcare coverage if they didn't like the free stuff they were getting here. That quieted them down for a while. But, as soon as the murmuring started up again, I decided to move my camp to another portion of the first floor, out of range of their barrage of bitching.

As I walked around a partition, sitting on a chair with no one around, was a black fedora. It was a prime example of a good felt hat, well made and sporting a silk band around the outside, with one of those nifty little bows attached to it.

. I examined the specimen closely. This fedora looked like it was brand new. I paid close attention to the inside sweat band, checking for the telltale signs of excessive hair-cream use and possible dandruff. As I spun this perfect example of the fedora trade around in my hands, my eyes fell on the little sizing tab. Lo and behold, it was my exact size, to within one-eighth of an inch. This was a gift from the powers that be in that unseen universe, the place where all perfectly good black fedoras originate.

Slowly, with the care of Humphrey Bogart, I placed the hat upon my head. The thing slid on like it had been made from a mold of my cranium — a perfect fit.

That hat immediately changed my personality. I went from being a number waiting in line to a real character, someone to be reckoned with on a dark night. I was the ultimate gangster, the fashionable man-about-town. My esteem level rose rapidly through my body and came to rest inside the dome of this magical fedora, creating an aura of intrigue, mystery, and all those other attributes of a well-dressed man.

Yes, my friend — I was *stylin'*.

When I reappeared in the pharmacy waiting-room area, the murmuring stopped. Eyes were averted. No one would look directly at me, though, look they did. *Who is this man of mystery?* That was the question on their collective faces. My image couldn't have been better served than with the addition of this black fedora.

I wore this hat for a few weeks. The thought of wearing it to bed crossed my mind, but better judgment won out, and I made that one concession. The magic black fedora sat strategically cocked on my head.

Man of mystery.

Then the itching started. There seemed to be this invisible ring of constant itch around my head. It required an admission of doubt before I associated my new black fedora with this plague upon my head. The scratching was getting so bad that I thought my hair would be pulled from my scalp. My fingertips became raw flesh from trying to relieve this scourge.

Finally, after a careful process of elimination, I arrived at the conclusion that my newfound fedora may very well be the source of the problem. There was nothing else left to blame.

It was with great pain that I realized that my Find of the Century was responsible for the itch on the top of my head. This beautiful black fedora was a black widow in disguise, a purveyor of doom and torment.

On my way to the VA Hospital to see a dermatologist, I carefully packed up the black fedora, with every intention of leaving it exactly where I'd found it. The doctor prescribed a number of medications and told me that I was suffering from a form of fungus. I corrected him. I said, "No, doctor. This isn't a fungus. This is pride being shattered on the stones of fate." Naturally, he looked at me like I had something growing out of my face, and then he returned to his prescription pad.

Afterwards, I had plenty of time to reflect on my mistake while waiting in the pharmacy area, listening, once again, to the old men complaining about everything in general.

The moral of this story, if there is a moral to be had, is quite simple: Beware of personality-changing gifts, no matter how they are acquired.

It has been more than 25 years since I donned that ill-gotten black fedora, and I'm still using the medicated shampoo that a number of doctors have prescribed for the scourge on the top of my head.

One Day at the Aerodrome

*M*ontego Bay, Jamaica, was one of my regular destinations back in my old university days in south Florida. It was an easy flight from Palm Beach or Fort Lauderdale International — a hop, skip, and a jump from south Florida.

I always booked the same small hotel, "Mrs. G's." I haven't a clue what the official name of the place was. I knew it only as "Mrs. G's." It was on the side of a hill, just out of Montego Bay proper, and in a nice tropical setting. A bunch of banana and palm trees surrounded the place, and the hill it sat upon was terraced.

Mrs. G was a very large black lady with an infectious laugh. I can still hear her as I write this. The room came with breakfast, which consisted of eggs and a lot of fresh fruit, very little meat. They had a nice small swimming pool built into the side of the mountain, where I used to spend my time trying to pick up the nice Catholic girl tourists.

Just down the hill, a few blocks into town, was a little store that had a huge selection of rum. That was why I went there, primarily — just to drink all kinds of rum. Some of my favorites were Mount Gay White and Appleton Superproof — the latter was 120-proof stuff. You had to be careful with Superproof; it was like rocket fuel.

This was back in the '70s when I was making these little sorties into Montego Bay. I would go and check in, and then run down and grab a few bottles of decent rum. Hell, the stuff was $1.25 a bottle back then — really cheap drinks. The most expensive things were the Cokes I had sent up to my room.

I would sit on the balcony, overlooking the valley, with all the banana trees around, daydreaming that I was Hemingway or Jack London. I would write pure rubbish on my Smith Corona "Traveler." Maybe it was some other model, but the thing weighed only 7 pounds, and it was really thin, so it fit really well into a suitcase or carry-on bag. I had this deerskin-leather bag that was perfect for a single-man-about-town to travel with, especially when you were going to Jamaica, where you didn't need an abundance of clothing. It was the tropics — a couple pairs of shorts and some T-shirts, and you were in business.

Well, every good thing must eventually come to a close, and that's what happened on this particular adventure. I ran out of money. No problem. I had my return ticket, and I could hitchhike once I got back to Florida.

What I hadn't counted on was the new airport tax. No one told me about this until I got to the Montego Bay International Airport. These two uniformed officers of the law asked me for the $2 US, and I didn't have it. They considered throwing me in jail but decided against it after I convinced them that I could borrow the money on the plane if they would let me get to it.

Finally, the two cops escorted me to the plane, and I went down the aisle, asking people for money. Panhandling on a 707 jetliner — it may have been a first; I don't know. My biggest concern was staying out of the Montego Bay lockup over a crummy two bucks.

Well, a Good Samaritan from Washington, DC, finally coughed up the two greenbacks, and I paid my dues. But the cops wouldn't leave the plane until they got ready to close the door. I guess they wanted to make sure I didn't sneak off that jet and run off into the jungle.

I got the guy's address and eventually sent him

the $2 — with a little interest — and thanked
him for keeping my ass out of jail.

On that trip, I had checked my bag. I can't
remember why I did this, but I do recall the fact
because of the little episode that occurred at the
Fort Lauderdale Airport.

There was a gaggle of US tourists wearing
pineapple shirts and fresh from the tropics of
sunny Jamaica gathered around the baggage
claim. Nothing was happening. Not a single
bag came out of the little trap door. Although
it was going around, it just wasn't delivering
the necessary freedom from the aerodrome that
everyone wanted. There must have been 200
people standing there waiting for their bags.

I was fortified with the last of my Appleton
Superproof Rum, smuggled onto the plane
after the ill-fated $2 tax debacle. Thus, I was
properly greased for any occasion. So I jumped
up on the stainless-steel rail and informed
everyone that I, Jason the Dauntless, the
Fearless, the Magnificent — and just rummed
up enough to blast all common inhibitions —
would ride this belt back into the bowels of
the airport and, God willing and with some
incredible luck, if I made it back, would report
on the status of our luggage.

So, that is what I did. I sat down on the

big rubber belt and rode back through the flappers hanging down, into the netherworld of baggage-land. As I emerged on the other side, like some ancient Greek warrior being delivered over the River Styx by Charon, I encountered this very large black man, who said, "Boy, what in the hell do you think you're doing?"

And I said, "Sir, I represent several hundred paying customers on the other side of that wall who would like to see their baggage, if you don't mind." I said this while sliding along, seated on the rubber belt.

The man informed me that it was on the way and to "…never — and I mean *never* — pull a stunt like this again."

As I emerged on the other side, in the land of the living once more, I duly informed my fellow passengers that the baggage was forthcoming. They gave me a standing ovation — mainly because everyone there was standing, anyway.

The Hero of Baggage Carousel Number 5 — that is what they called me: A Greek Warrior of the Modern World.

Juicy Lucy

*A*s kids, my brothers and I grew up on the side of a mountain. Our house was exactly one mile up the side of Larksville Mountain. Please keep in mind that the town of Larksville was very small. It had one main street — Wilson Street, undoubtedly named after President Woodrow Wilson. The town had a tailor named "Stanley" — hence the name "Stanley's Tailor Shop." There was a small theater called "The Lark," a little cigar-and-penny-candy store named after its owners, "Kiltey's," an assortment of gin mills, a small restaurant — and probably a few other establishments lost in the residue of time and my aging memory. On the top of the hill, where Wilson Street turned into Jackson Street, was a church named after a guy named "Stanislaus." It served the people whose names ended in "-sky," "-ski," and "-ziwec."

Halfway up the mountain were the strip mines. These were exactly what the name implies — big holes in the ground where the coal companies "stripped" off the top of the earth to uncover the coal buried below. There used to be a thriving coal-mining industry in this area. It was of the deep-mine variety and employed quite a few people. But sheer greed ruined all that with the Fort Knox Mine Disaster, which occurred in 1957. You can look it up if you wish. It spelled the death of the anthracite coal industry in Wyoming Valley. I won't go there today because it is depressing as hell.

We had only one neighbor to speak of. My Aunt Alice and Uncle Lester Cornilius lived below us on 22 acres of land. They had two daughters, named Sharon and Little Alice. While the girls were still very young, the family pulled up stakes and moved to Fort Lauderdale, Florida. Back in the 1950s, that was the land of golden opportunity. Plus, my Uncle Lester didn't like the winters in Pennsylvania.

There was some bad blood between Alice and my dad. It was a given that he would acquire the 22 acres of land that she owned. Something happened between Aunt Alice and my dad, to which we kids weren't privy. In most cases of

this type, the adults never tell the kids the real
truth about what had happened — you only
heard rumors. But the bottom line was that she
sold the land to someone else, a couple named
Al and Lucy Bowman.

Listen — I'm aware that using the term
"Juicy" to describe Mrs. Bowman might be in
questionable taste, but what can I say? That
was her nickname, and I didn't see any reason
not to use it. She'd been known as "Juicy Lucy"
since time began.

You could say that Al and Lucy were late
bloomers. They didn't have any children until
we were all grown up and had moved away.
So, back then, we were her surrogate kids, you
might say.

Lucy was crazy about all of us — although,
for some reason that only human attraction can
fully explain, she especially liked yours truly.
Whenever we would visit, she would make iced
graham crackers. They were to die for — large
regular graham crackers covered with vanilla
cake icing, which Lucy would really heap on.
Man, that was a treat.

Everything would have been perfectly "Leave
It to Beaver" stuff, except for one thing. Juicy
Lucy always wore copious amounts of red
lipstick. She probably still does to this day. It

was the fire-engine-red variety. As I walked
toward their back door with my cherished
and coveted iced graham cracker in hand, she
would plant this huge red kiss on the side of
my face — she would literally grab me and give
me this gooey, all-day red kiss. She did this
for years. If I saw her today, I'd wager that she
would try to kiss me.

  As a kid, I would walk around Larksville
Mountain, a real he-man, with a giant red kiss
on the side of my face.

A Day at the Beach

*M*y wife and I spent a couple of years in Key West, Florida. She had taken a job slinging fried-fish sandwiches at the Half Shell Raw Bar, and I worked as a heavy-equipment operator for two local firms, Toppino's and Clarence Keevan and Son.

At that time — and I have no reason to believe anything has changed — Florida was a "Right to Work" state. What that meant was that they never wanted to hear the word "union," and, as one old man once told me, "…half your pay is the sunshine…."

Even though I was a card-carrying member of the AFL-CIO/Operating Engineers, the Cadillac of labor unions, it didn't mean squat. I was paid $7 an hour and was told I was lucky to have a job. One day, old man Toppino told me, "We could hire a Haitian at $4 an hour to do your job, boy!" That was in 1985. All I could think about was that, in 1975, I'd been earning $15 an hour plus full benefits in Boulder, Colorado.

But we survived and managed to live well despite the poor labor relations at my place of employment, although one thing happened that has troubled me to this day. Hence, I will mention it.

It was a Thursday evening, and I was at home with my paycheck, sipping on a cold Colt 45 malt liquor, thinking about the fact that I'd just worked 12 hours in the 95-degree heat. We worked 7 days a week, 6:00 am to 6:00 pm every day. That's an 84-hour work week if you do the math. There I was, looking at the figure on my paycheck after taxes: $628 — that is what was typed on my check. My take-home pay, after working 84 hours in the summer heat of Key West, was $628!

A few hours later, my wife came home from her shift at the Raw Bar. She had worked a 6-hour shift that day. After she added up all of her cash tips, the amount came to $426 — in cash — not to mention her $2.36 per hour base pay. I had to ask myself: *What the hell am I doing wrong?*

Finally, after working 7 days per week, our boss was told that his men would perform better if they had a day off once in a while. His friend said that it would "increase productivity."

I wasn't going to complain and really didn't have an opinion either way. After working 12-hour days, 7 days per week, you become quite numb to controversy. I was just grateful that I didn't have to get up and go to work on Sunday anymore.

Well, at least until old man Toppino got behind on his contracts.

At the tip of the island of Key West is an area called The Truman Annex, where Harry Truman had his "Winter White House" during his tenure in office as President. My company sent me down there with a Caterpillar D-3 bulldozer with the instructions to clean up the small beach. I had to push all of the seaweed up on a pile for the trucks and payloader so that they could haul it away.

During the course of my workday, I realized that this was a nice little beach. It was shaded by Australian Pines, and it had a really nice feel to it — small and intimate. It was then that I decided to bring Teresa down there on my next day off, which would have been the following Sunday — a little R&R before the crushing work week started all over again. The place wasn't populated with screaming kiddies and coconut-smelling tourists asking me if I lived there.

Sure enough, the very next Sunday, we packed a basket of sandwiches and cold drinks (like I needed another sandwich in my life at that point) and headed off to the beach in my huge Pontiac Catalina.

Just several miles off the point is where the Dry Tortugas are located. This is where Dr. Mudd spent a holiday at the behest of the US government after President Lincoln was shot. We could almost see the red-brick prison out there on the horizon.

So we swam around a little, drank some soda, and ate a sandwich. Then we just lay out on our beach blanket, relaxing in the dappled sunlight. I was almost asleep when I heard a very faint noise. It was the sound of sand and stones moving. This beach wasn't the best as far as sand was concerned — in fact, it was pretty bad; there were a lot of rocks. When I'd bulldozed it, I backed out into the water a ways, trying to dredge up what little sand there was and place it in the spot that I was planning to occupy that Sunday.

Anyway, I heard a little splash and glanced up from my repose. As I raised my head, I almost lost my lunch and an entire week of dinner at what I saw.

There, emerging from the water, were a half-dozen "frogmen," all dressed in black, carrying all sorts of weapons — hand grenades, bowie knives, and all of the equipment you'd need to go exploring the ocean depths. They were almost silent — no noise, no talking. They were just crawling on their bellies right up to our blanket — nothing on them rattled or made any noise whatsoever. They quietly wriggled up the beach, and, when they'd reached our position, they parted into two groups, as if to surround my encampment. Not a word was spoken. My first thought was trying to remember if I'd paid for my parking space or not.

As it turned out, they were Navy SEALS engaged in what Navy SEALS do on their days off — go around appearing out of the ocean and scaring the living crap out of underpaid equipment operators and their overpaid wives.

This was simply a training exercise and had absolutely nothing to do with my not paying for parking. Hell, I knew the attendant from when I worked down there, and he'd let me in for nothing.

I didn't know the government was that hard up for cash!

Buddy, You Know How to Eat!

*D*o you know what the ulnar nerve is?
Well, I didn't — until mine started acting
up. I was losing all sensation in my left hand,
especially in my fingers. So, I went to the VA
hospital in Wilkes-Barre, Pennsylvania, and
had them look at it. They did the x-rays and
a consult. They called it an "impaction of
my ulnar nerve on the left elbow" and told
me I needed surgery. But they didn't do that
there, and, so, they sent me to their facility in
Manhattan, on 28th Street.

The time came, and I went to New York.
They drove me down there in a van with a few
other veterans seeking help in the Big Apple.
The staff there explained that they used the
"Hoptel" system. A "Hoptel" is a cross between
a "hospital" and a "hotel." What it amounts to
is this: If your surgery is simple, they put you
up for the night in a plain room on campus
— no nursing or meals, just a room. You sleep

there, and then they come at 5:00 am and take you into surgery, perform the operation, and discharge you to a waiting van for the ride home.

It had been years since I'd bombed around Manhattan, so I decided to take a cab over to Little Italy and have dinner at one of my favorite Italian restaurants, Puglia's. It's been there for many years, and it's a great spot, one which I'd highly recommend.

I had the entire late afternoon and evening to myself, so I told the waiter that I didn't want to be rushed. I said that I would make it worth his while to just allow me to take my sweet time eating dinner, and he agreed.

I started out with some nice antipasto, then some espresso, and then on to the clams casino, then a few more tidbits, then more espresso, and then came the main event.

You're probably getting the obvious picture. I sat there, at a sidewalk table, for the better part of three hours, having dinner. It was fantastic.

Just when the waiter was bringing my check, a guy came out of the bar across the street. He walked diagonally across the street and came right up to me. This is what he said:

"Buddy, youse know howda eat. We've been sitting over dere for the last three hours, watching you. I just won 5 bucks on a bet because youse really know howda eat."

With that, he turned and walked back to the bar.

I tipped the waiter well, called a cab, and went back to my hoptel room, satisfied.

Pain Management

*W*hile living in Charleston, South
Carolina, I had a few issues with chronic pain.
Please understand, I'm still dealing with that
same malady — chronic pain — to this day,
and through the use of creative medications
and working out at the gym, I have been able to
keep most of the problems at bay.

But, back then, I didn't have too many
alternatives. I started seeing a father-and-son
team of pain doctors at Roper Hospital, located
in downtown Charleston. Their approach was
the use of injections directly into the lower back
— into the spinal column, to be exact. I would
go there, and they would inject a combination
of steroids and pain medication into my back.
I would then be placed in a hospital bed for
about two hours, until I could feel my legs
again — or walk, for that matter.

One day, Dr. Ivester injected me with his
cocktail of medical juices, and I was duly sent

into the ward to wait until the effects wore
off. But, on this occasion, something different
happened. As I lay there, I noticed that my
stomach was getting numb. Then the numbness
proceeded to creep up into my chest. Alarmed,
I called the nurse over and explained that
something was radically wrong. She, in turn,
summoned the doctor. He took one look at me
and went into red alert.

They injected me with all kinds of stuff, and
then they just waited. As it turned out, he had
shot me in the back a little higher than normal.
The medications started running up instead of
down and started to numb everything, right
up to my neck. He told me that, if they hadn't
caught that in time, it would have stopped my
breathing and then my heart.

Ooooops!

Just a little mistake, there, Mr. Goodman.

In effect, what happened was that I was turned
into a chemically induced paraplegic. I was
simply a head resting on a pillow for more
than four hours. I couldn't feel anything in my
entire body — just the pressure of my head
on the pillow. It was strange, and it gave me a
thorough understanding of what that feels like
— to be a total paraplegic. I have placed that
right up there near the top of my list of life's

strange experiences.

Another item on that list was a full-color view of my lower GI tract during a colonoscopy. My doctor gave me a scope and allowed me to view the blockage. He also printed out full-color glossies of that image for my scrapbook. Today, when someone calls me an asshole, I can correct them and show them what I really look like inside.

Getting back to the original story: Connected to Roper Hospital was this brand-new, 21-day inpatient pain clinic. That's what it was called: "The Pain Clinic." Dr. Ivester decided that I might benefit from a 21-day exposure to what they had to offer; so, I was enrolled into their program.

This deal sucked from the very start. You must understand that I am, unfortunately, very hospital savvy. It comes from spending so much time in those places. After 27 major surgeries, you begin to understand what hospitals are all about.

I knew something wasn't quite right with this "Pain Clinic" from the very start, but I couldn't put my finger on it. It was just a feeling that not everything was the way it was supposed to be.

Anyway, I went through this bogus program, and, as it turned out, their answer to everything was a cup full of frozen ice. They would fill a Styrofoam cup with water and freeze it. Then you peeled the Styrofoam away to expose the ice. They said to rub the area until it went numb.

I developed a hot, burning pain in my lower back, on the left side. It was pretty bad — a really hot, singeing type of pain.

So I kept telling them that I needed an x-ray or something. I knew that there was something wrong — hell, I just happen to live in this body 24/7 and know a little about the way it works. But their answer was always the same: Just rub it with a cup of ice. No narcotic pain medication — just a cup of frozen H_2O. Period.

This went on for the last week to 10 days of my stay. As soon as I was discharged, I flew up to Scranton, Pennsylvania, and was checked into my old alma mater, CMC Hospital. This was where a "Dr. Black" had done most of my lower-back surgeries.

They did a bunch of examinations and x-rays and then immediately prepped me for surgery. I was wheeled into the Operating Room, and the doc did his thing. As it turned out, I was under for a few hours, and they removed this large tumor from my back. He said it was the size of a baseball and had grown out of the nerve endings down there. It had one of those big, long medical names.

I spent a week in the hospital with this drain in my back, because the hole that this thing had left was big. Finally, they were able to patch me up enough to send me home to Charleston.

A day or two after I landed, I went by to see the people at "The Pain Clinic." It was perfect. I couldn't have asked for a better arrangement. The two guys who ran this debauchery were personally testing out a new device that was actually an old-fashioned "rack." The boss man was strapped into the thing and couldn't move. You might say he was in the process of being stretched out.

Well, I hiked up my shirt. The height of the table was just right. I turned around and shoved this big, stapled, oozing scar right in his face and said, "Here. Look at this. Is this 'in my head'? Do you think a little cup of ice will fix this thing? Well, do you, punk?" (That was inspired by Clint Eastwood.)

Naturally, he was grossed out and almost puked on his brand-new, old-fashioned rack device.

But I made my point. Those bastards had made me walk around in terrible pain for two weeks.

About two years later, we were living back in

Pennsylvania, and a friend sent me a newspaper clipping. As it turned out, both father and son were frauds. No medical degrees, no licenses, no nothing but a lot of greed. Their "Pain Clinic" was a big insurance-ripoff facility. When they went to cuff these pricks, they shot through and escaped. Someone had tipped them off, and they fled the state.

Eventually, they were caught, and they both did time. I still smile when I think of the look on his face when I shoved that big, oozing scar into it.

Juvenile Delinquency, Revisited

In 1965, I was 15 years old. Because my Dad had bought my brothers their first cars, I was afraid that he would buy me a four-door Buick or some other disastrous-model automobile. A rising star in the world of Greaserhood couldn't be seen driving around in some square car. I wanted to be a hot-rodder. It was that simple.

So I went out and bought a 1955 Ford Crown Victoria. This was a special car. If I had that thing today in good nick, it would probably be worth a ton of money.

The car was black, and I installed a 312-cubic-inch "Police Interceptor" engine in it with a big Holley four-barrel carburetor. This car could haul ass.

I spent the entire year up to my 16th birthday working on this car. I did everything to it — not just the engine. I put cherry-bomb mufflers under it. I jacked it up in front. I sent the front seat out to have it "rolled and tucked" — an upholstering technique that was the "in" thing back then.

The final application was to paint the words *The Bounty* on the rear bumper. Don't ask. It was in vogue to "name" your car, so I called mine *The Bounty.*

Finally, the big day arrived. I could drive legally on my 16th birthday. Man, I was cool. A big black Ford "Crown Vic," as it was called, with a big hunk of chrome going over the roof, baby-moon hubcaps on black-painted wheels with wide whitewall tires. The cat's meow.

I did a little street racing with the thing and blew off mainly Chevies. If the guy couldn't shift, I could beat a 327-cubic-inch Chevy any day. Mostly, I blew off the 283s.

In high school, only a few of us had cars. Joe Hogan was a classmate and future rival. He owned a black, six-cylinder Chevy BelAir, a four-door, the exact car I didn't want my Dad to buy me. Joe would always insist on trying to beat my big Ford, and he just couldn't do it. He was outclassed, but I had to give him credit for trying — and try he did. This went on for years, even after we graduated. I would see him around town years later, and he would always ask me what I was driving.

One night, Joe tried to outrun me on a wide street — Washington Avenue — in Plymouth, Pennsylvania. The movie *AWOL* did a fair job of demonstrating what an armpit Plymouth, Pennsylvania, really was, in case you're interested.

I was busy kicking his ass when I heard the cop-car siren.

Please understand: Our father was a big-shot business owner in those parts. We did trucking and excavating, and everyone who wasn't pushing up daisies knew who the Goodmans were. This applied to the police, also. They knew my car. Hell! — how many jet-black Ford Crown Victorias were around that patch of scrub pine? One. Mine.

They gave up the chase for two reasons: One, they had a six-cylinder Chevy, just like Joey Hogan's. Two, they knew who I was and where I lived, so why bust a sweat?

I pulled into our driveway and parked. I was on my way to the house when the cops showed up. They didn't give me a ticket, but they did give me a lecture and told me all of the things I'd done wrong. Unknown to me, my father was standing in his bedroom window, listening to the entire diatribe. So I "Yes'd" them to death and apologized all over the place. I would have groveled if need be, even though I was an up-and-coming Juvenile Delinquent and all.

Finally, after what seemed like an hour, they got into their squad car and left. I wiped my brow and thought, *I just dodged a bullet.* Then I proceeded to walk around the back of my house to go to bed. Just when I was ready to open the screen door, a huge fist came out and decked me in the chops. I fell backwards onto my ass.

Standing there, looking through the busted screen door, was my old man. He was wearing his boxer shorts with the red hearts on them, and his face was just as red as the hearts were. He pointed at me and said, "Tomorrow, you sell that car, or you don't drive!" He turned and went back into his bedroom.

It was an idle threat, really. I drove one of his coal trucks, so the thought of me not driving was going to lose him a lot of money — and I knew he would never let that happen. I assume — probably correctly — that he was secretly pissed off because I hadn't allowed him to buy me a really dull car, and his greatest fears had been realized. I was turning into a real Juvenile Delinquent.

Jelly Donut and Trust

*A*llow me to relate a little cautionary tale about the concept of Unconditional Trust.

Now, I am not a religious man by any stretch of the imagination. Some people would see me as an agnostic. There was a time when I did study for several years about religion, so allow me to tell you about that.

It was my fourth major back surgery. The doctor who worked on me had "nicked" my spinal column — his term. This resulted in my spinal fluid dripping out of my back. If it had all leaked out, I ran the risk of being paralyzed from the lower back down. To remedy this grievous situation, they strapped me to the bed, and I remained that way for 37 days. I could raise my head only 22 degrees.

I have always been an avid reader, so, once I was placed in my new hospital bed and the straps were in place, I was jonesing for something to read. I reached around and felt

the end table. In the drawer was a copy of
The Good News Bible. When I opened the front
cover, this sentence jumped off the page at me:
"What will you tell God when he asks you the
question, 'Did you read My book?'"

Well, I was dumbfounded. Being a published
author, I could relate to the ego attached to an
author's first book. So, I thought about all the
trashy books I'd read in my life. I had never
read *That One Book.* But the pain and duress
over my back condition launched me on a
six-year quest to study all the major religions
of the world. After all of that study, none of
them still didn't make much sense to me, but I
did discover that they all shared one common
thread, one common underlying factor: They
were all based on Unconditional Trust!

Now, I'm going to tell you how I was
introduced to the concept of "Unconditional
Trust" and its deeper significance and meaning.

It was the early 1970s, and I was a student
at Florida Atlantic University in Boca Raton,
Florida. I had a friend there named Rick Shaw.
He was from Oak Ridge, Tennessee, and he was
a good picker and grinner. In other words, he
played banjo and guitar, and sang with another
guy around town. One place they played was
called The Gathering Place.

It was a small lounge not far from campus. Please understand that, at that time in south Florida, there was a lot of competition in the gin-mill business. They all came up with different gimmicks to get you to drink booze in their establishment. One of those tricks was the use of a "gong." When the gong rang out, whatever you were drinking, they would line up three or four in front of you, no extra charge. This was great at the time — a cheap high. I was in my Black Russian phase at the time, so, "Gong!" and there would be four more of the dirty little buggers in front of me.

Naturally, it stood to reason that I would get blasted. "The Gathering Place" was a meat market. It was the kind of lounge you frequented to drink, listen to music, and get laid.

I ended up at the house of some woman one morning. I had no idea how I'd gotten there. All I knew is that I was naked, lying in bed, with a strange woman next to me. Her back was turned toward me, so I never even knew what she looked like.

When I rolled over the other way, I was given a start. There was this little boy — no more than three or four years old — blond hair, blue eyes, holding a jelly donut with a huge chomp out of it. The kid held up his donut and said, "Want a bite of my donut, Daddy?"

Needless to say, I was mortified. Here I am buck naked, lying in bed with this kid's mother, a perfect stranger, and he is offering me a bite of his jelly donut.

After I used a pillow to "hide my shame" (like they said about Adam and Eve), I found my clothes, poured the kid some milk from the fridge, and then went out to look for my automobile.

After I sobered up a bit, I started thinking about this incident. This was the purest definition of the term "unconditional trust."

This I applied many years later, after reading all the Bibles, Korans, and other Good Books: you have to have unconditional trust to make any of it work in your life.

I am still searching for that trust to this day.

Dropping the Ball(s)

*I*n my book *Urban Gothic,* I recounted a few tales of the sea relating to my experience as a member of the U.S. Navy. Well, here's another one of those sea stories.

Onboard the ship I crewed back from Vietnam on was a Lieutenant Junior Grade who hated my guts. You will have to read those other stories from *Urban Gothic* to understand how this state of affairs had come about. It would take too much time to explain it here. Suffice it to say that this guy didn't like me and that the feeling was pretty much mutual.

We steamed across the Pacific Ocean and stopped in Guam, and then we continued on to Hawaii. I saved up my liberty and used five days of it drinking and getting laid on Waikiki Beach. One night, I met this guy who sold me some really good LSD. It was called "Strawberry Fields," and it was dynamite. If I had known in advance it was that good, I would have bought

50 hits of the stuff. However, as is the case with all hindsight, I purchased only four pills.

The guy who sold it to me had an interesting story. He was in Hawaii hiding from the cops. As it turned out, his father, who happened to be a judge in Austin, Texas, had sentenced him to 20 years in jail for the crime of possession of marijuana. Twenty freakin' years. His own kid. Man, talk about Hardcore Harry here. I had every reason to believe him because he had sold me some honest LSD.

The last day I spent in Hawaii, I was pulling duty aboard the tub we called a "Man-o-War," *The Luzerne County* LST 902. The Navy actually had boats designated "LSD," also! The Officer of the Day was — you guessed it — Mr. Wonderful, my nemesis, The Lieutenant from Hell.

Just to bust my salty balls, this guy ordered me to go down into the belly of the ship and carry every piece of sports equipment up to his office for him to examine. It was called "The Sports Locker," and, when I opened this thing up, it was crammed with every kind of ball stuff you could imagine. I mean a load of stuff here: baseball bats, gloves, and, especially, the balls. There were at least 12 volleyballs alone. Not to mention the softballs, basketballs, and every other piece of crap you could blow air into.

As it happened, at the time I received these orders, I was tripping my ass off. This stuff was good — no doubt about that. Because we were taking rolls of up to 35 degrees for days on end, I felt like the ship was still rolling like crazy, even though we were snuggly tied to the pier. Besides my perceived rolling sensation, the nuke boys in their submarine were testing their sonar device across the harbor. This sounded like some giant, slamming the side of the ship with a huge sledgehammer.

With the motion and the cacophony of noise going on — not to mention the numerous ladders and steps that I had to navigate to get this crap up to officers' country — it was one mixed-up affair. Naturally the LSD only enhanced all of this. The stupid steps were like putty, and they kept undulating under my feet. Plus, I kept dropping the bag of balls, and they would go rolling down the passageway in all different colors. It was just a visual and auditory treat to the senses.

Finally, I got a bag of basketballs up to his office. I'd left a trail of balls all over the ship in my wake. He looked at me and knew that something wasn't quite right. He even sniffed my breath to see if I'd been drinking, but he couldn't figure it out. The fact that my pupils looked like peanut-butter jar lids didn't help matters in the least.

You could say that I was dropping the balls on that particular occasion.

Shaken, Not Stirred

*A*ustralia always appealed to me. And, in 1976, I was given an opportunity to explore that country "Down Under." At the time, I was studying toward a Master's degree in Art Education at Florida Atlantic University in Boca Raton, Florida. One day while I was walking down a corridor there, I stumbled upon a flyer offering teaching jobs in Australia.

As it turned out, they were interviewing people in Madison, Wisconsin; so I flew up there, had an interview, and got the job.

Within months, I was on my way to Australia to teach art in their secondary schools.

There are a few generalities that struck me about living and working in Australia. First of all, everything has venom of some sort. Secondly, Australians really do not like Americans. When I would attend cocktail parties or their famous bar-b-ques, after a few pops, the snide jokes would start. They would start by calling me a "Septic Tank." This was a bastardization of the term "Yank." Many of the older guys would use "Yank" because they'd served in "The Big One" — World War Two. The younger generation, however, didn't have that allegiance to the United States. The only reason I could discern as to why they felt this way was this: we worked.

Australians love to party. They viewed work as a necessary evil — just something to pay for the "snags" (sausages and beer). We Americans — as well as the Germans — didn't mind working a full, eight-hour day and completing the task at hand. Australians didn't look at it that way, and, so, an animosity developed.

Look: I realize that this is a gross generality, but it was the mid-'70s, and I lived there, so it was my sole observation. I know what I'm saying — I got into a major fistfight in Tasmania over this same subject, but that's another story.

Speaking of stories, over time, I found myself befriending more people from New Zealand. They were warm, genuine people who suffered the same fate as Americans: they weren't liked in Australia, either. One of these friends was my doctor. He was a young guy struggling to make a buck, and I used his services.

One day I was in the shower, "examining my stuff," as they used to say. I realized that I had these ugly warts on the underside — or *down under,* if you please — of my penis. This, I decided, was not a condition I could tolerate. I was young and single, and I made a lot of money. I *needed* my equipment to be in top-notch shape in order to accommodate these Aussie women.

I called the Doc and went to see him. After his initial examination, he sat back and said, "Why do you want to take them off? These act like a French Tickler."

He proceeded to explain that they were plantar's warts and that they were fairly common in men. He said he could remove them with a few dabs of liquid nitrogen.

Well, I held my old Johnson up while the good doctor opened his stainless-steel thermos bottle; the vapors flowed out like an old horror movie. He dabbed at my plantar's warts with this substance, chilled as it was to some ridiculous amount of degrees below zero.

After the applications, he told me to get dressed while he sat and wrote a prescription for some salve to put on the site.

In conversation, he mentioned this: "Jason, you may experience some excruciating pain later on. For some reason, there is a delayed reaction, and, several hours from now, you may have significant pain down there."

That evening, I was supposed to attend a very highbrow cocktail party with the officials of the school district. They were serving canapés and drinks in some ballroom in downtown Melbourne. It wasn't the type of function that I could easily bow out of — I had to be there.

So I asked the doctor what I should do if this attack of serious pain were to afflict my dick, and he told me this:

"The only suggestion that I can give you is this: Soak your penis in a glass filled with ice cubes. Use a rock glass if you have one. They seem to work well for this purpose."

At first, I thought he was making a reference to the size of my manhood.

Use a rock glass, my ass. I'll need a large tumbler, at least.

Then I told him that I would look a little ridiculous at this *hoi polloi* cocktail party with my dick in a glass on the rocks.

His only comment was, "Don't forget the wedge of lime."

The Peppermint Twist

*L*ately, I've been reading a lot about our fearless president wanting to privatize everything — supposedly to save taxpayers money. But everything seems to point to the opposite outcome once these companies get their hands on our air traffic control system, our local utilities, and our water supply. I *live* in a town that has sold the rights to its water supply to an outside company. This for-profit firm has taken over our water system, which consists of a series of deep wells that supply the town of Lititz, Pennsylvania.

Every year, they are required by law to send me a report concerning the water quality. After I received the first water-quality report, I went out and invested in a set of filters for my entire house. This is a system that uses both primary and secondary filtration; the secondary filters have active charcoal in them, and they work very well. My filters take out everything, even the taste of chlorine. I don't have to worry about any bacterial infestations, like the one that attacked Milwaukee several years ago.

Lititz uses the combined water of four deep wells. One of these wells happens to be located just south of the huge Johnson & Johnson plant up the street on West Lincoln Avenue. This plant, which makes a variety of household products, employs a considerable number of people in this town.

During one particular stretch of time, they were making peppermint mouthwash. An article appeared in the local newspaper that dealt with a mysterious occurrence: All of the water in Lititz seemed to have a peppermint aftertaste. Now, I never noticed this, because of the filters I mentioned earlier, but a number of my friends told me about it. This peppermint aftertaste lasted for about three days.

Lo and behold, they find out that Johnson & Johnson just happened to have been making peppermint mouthwash for those same three days.

Hmmmm…. What an interesting coincidence.

When the powers-that-be approached Johnson & Johnson, they immediately denied any wrongdoing. They refused to accept any culpability for any action and flat-out said that they had nothing to do with this. In essence, they told the town of Lititz's officials to go fly a kite — or something to that effect.

Naturally, with a few hundred jobs at stake, no one was really going to argue the point.

Let's just say that the people of Lititz have the nicest breath of any town on the East Coast.

I Showed Him...

*T*here was a time in my life when I was young and stupid. Now that I'm older, I feel just old and stupid. But that isn't what this story is about.

Or is it?

Back in the day (I hate that expression, for some reason), I was enrolled in a two-year degree program at my local community college. I studied Art and Advertising, and, eventually, I went on to earn an Associate's degree.

Though most of my courses were electives, I still had to study a program of compulsory curriculum. There was some math, history, social studies, and, of course, English.

At that time, I was living the life of a chameleon. During the day, I was the Student Body President, President of the Rotary Club on campus two years in a row, an honor student, and all-around Mister Big Shot. At night, I turned into either a hippy-dippy LSD dealer or a suave playboy type who haunted the local cocktail lounges looking for girls.

My partner in the LSD business was a guy named Louie. He and I would drive out to Boston or down to Hell's Kitchen in Manhattan and buy shoebox quantities of Orange Barrel or Purple Micro Dot acid. Then we'd transport our wares up to Wilkes-Barre, add a substantial markup, and distribute it around the four college campuses in our area. It was a very lucrative business, to say the least.

One night, Louie and I "financed" the showing of The Beatles' movie *Yellow Submarine* at a theatre in downtown Wilkes-Barre. We didn't put up the money per se. We supplied the LSD for all of the paying patrons and the public.

Man, you should have seen the results. In the city of Wilkes-Barre, there is a "square" — a park-like area surrounded on all four sides by major thoroughfares. When the movie got out, most of the crowd just wandered into that park area to continue their trip. The authorities knew that something was wrong but just couldn't figure out what that could be. It was great.

Getting back to the story, well, you could say that I was a "rebel without a cause" to some degree. I protested against authority just like any other kid who was ever 18 years old. That meant that I did some things that verged on the level of anti-social.

For a while, I carried a portable cassette player. Do you remember those? The things weighed a ton and weren't really that small, but they did operate on "C" cell batteries, which validated the title of "portable."

I had this class — English 101. Now, I didn't have anything against England or their language at that time. I just didn't like the instructor. This guy was boring as hell, and he would just disappear from time to time. Our college was located on the river common, a grassy strip hard by the banks of the Susquehanna River that had some nice trees for shade and benches for people to sit on. If it was a nice day, this instructor would keep staring out the windows and lose his train of thought while he was in the middle of his lecture. Then he'd tell us to write a 1,000-word essay on something or other, and then, he'd just leave. One day, we followed him and found the guy asleep under one of those big trees!

One day, I was in the men's room, and I flushed the toilet. The sound was incredible.

It sounded like a submarine had just blown its ballast tanks right there in the room. So, I got out my trusty "portable" cassette player, slammed in a blank tape, and taped the sound of that toilet flush.

A few hours later, I was sitting in this boring English Composition class, wondering why I was exposing myself to all of this rot. Then, I remembered the toilet-flush tape.

I cued it up, stood up, and announced, "Here's what I think of your lectures!" Then I hit the "Play" button on the unit, and everyone could hear this loud *Whoosh! Gurgle! Gurgle! Bah-Flusshh!* It filled the room with a cacophony of brilliant noise. Then, I made a spectacle of myself by stomping out of the classroom.

He never really said anything to me until it was the end of the semester, and the grades came out. He gave me a "D" in English Composition 101.

Now, a "D" grade is actually a passing grade, but you can't transfer it to another college. So, it was basically useless.

I ended up going to summer school to make up that course. And, sure enough, when I showed up for my first class that summer, guess who the instructor was: Yep! The same guy.

   After a lot of ass kissing and begging, I finally ended up with a passing and transferable grade.

   You could say that *I showed him....*

Fingerwork

*I*n Vietnam, I was stationed aboard a U.S. Navy vessel called an "LST." This small boat was used during World War Two to land tanks onto the beach in the Pacific Theatre. In fact, LST 902 was built for basically just one landing — on Okinawa. They didn't expect it to survive due to Japan's *Kamikaze* attacks. This boat was a piece of crap.

We supplied ammunition and beer to all the small firebases along the Mekong River. It was pretty hazardous duty because the NVA and the Viet Cong didn't want to see all that ordnance get to its destination.

On one particular trip up the river, we stopped in an area known as Ving Long, Long Bin, or, sometimes, even as Suc Dic. I can't remember the exact location; hell, it was more than 50 years ago. But I do remember the following story.

I went off on my own. It was a way of

maintaining my sanity — going off by myself
for a few hours and really looking at the
countryside. They assured me that it was
relatively safe, that the area had been cleared
of hostiles. So I grabbed a little motorbike
rickshaw and headed out.

I came upon this small town, and, as I
entered, I could see the evidence of a major
confrontation. The earth was pockmarked with
bomb craters. All of the buildings had large-
caliber-machinegun holes in them. But life went
on as usual.

My taxi dropped me off in front of this small
hotel. When I walked in, I strolled through the
bar, through the whorehouse, and finally came
out on a patio of sorts that was built right over
the Mekong River. This was the restaurant. It
was a beautiful place.

As I sat there waiting for my food to arrive,
a group of young girls came out and occupied
a table in the corner. I think they may have
been the employees of the whorehouse that
I mentioned, just taking a break from the
rigors of their profession. It was then that I
understood why they told me that the place
was secure. It was the whorehouse, dummy! Of
course, our guys are going to fight their heads
off. This area had to be liberated from the Viet

Cong for obvious reasons!

Finally, my dinner arrived, and I started looking around for my silverware.

There wasn't any. The only eating implement they placed in front of me was a pair of chopsticks.

There I was, literally *stabbing* my food and trying to get it into my mouth. All the while, these girls were over there, laughing their cute little "asses for hire" off. Eventually, one of the girls got up and walked over to my table — still laughing her ass off. She positioned my fingers in the correct configuration so that I could manipulate the chopsticks.

Not a word was spoken, which was understandable: I didn't speak Vietnamese, and they didn't speak English.

To this very day, I still employ that technique when using chopsticks. Whenever my wife and I go to our favorite sushi place, I use only chopsticks.

And I owe that to a few little girls in a remote village in Vietnam.

Fabric Softeners

I enlisted in the U.S. Navy back in 1968. At that time, the Navy was all about tradition. We wore the famous "Bell Bottom" pants with the 13 buttons on the front. They proved to be a challenge if you allowed the call of nature to go unheeded.

My "rate," as they called it, was that of a boatswain's mate. I did everything there was to do on the main deck of the ship — "above the water line," you could say.

When I went through boot camp at the Great Lakes facility, we had to wash all of our clothes at these huge marble washtubs, scrubbing them up and down on the abrasive surface until all of the stains came out of our dress-white uniforms.

Then, the really interesting part took place.

Between the barracks were these clotheslines. A lot of history hung on those babies, I can tell you that. But do you think the Navy would

use ordinary wooden clothespins, like the
rest of the world? Not exactly. They had these
little pieces of rope. The things were about 12
inches long and had little metal ends crimped
on them. We had to *tie* all of our clothes on the
line.

But there was a particular *way* you had to
tie the pieces of clothes to the line. You just
couldn't do it all willy-nilly, or you'd get your
ass kicked. The ropes had to be all the same,
with a little bow in each, so that, when it hung
down, the officers could look through them. It
reminded me of the story in Greek myth that
had Ulysses shooting an arrow through axe
heads in order to get his wife and wine cellars
back. The officers had to be able to see straight
down the line of bows to the very end — or
else!

Well, that was exemplary of the level of
tradition in the Navy. We had work clothes.
A pair of denim pants and a light-blue shirt.
Actually, two pair and one long-sleeved shirt
and another short-sleeved model. But you never
called them "blue jeans." That was *verboten.*
They were referred to as "denim work trousers."

I have always hated to wear brand-new
clothes. I don't care what the article was. It had
to be washed several thousand times before I

could wear it with any semblance of comfort. The same held true when I was in the Navy. New clothes drove me crazy.

In Vietnam, because of the heat, humidity, and the amount of sweating that we did, our clothes didn't last very long. They would practically rot off your back. Most of my work uniforms were all shot — no pun intended — when we were ordered out of Vietnam. Now, keep in mind that there was a "sea bag" aboard. Maybe it was called a "sea chest." I can't really remember, but that's not important. I will describe it. It was this big hamper filled with old clothes. You could go in there and grab some old shirts if need be and wear them.

One day, I was on deck in Vietnam. I was wearing a blue work shirt, boosted from the sea bag/sea chest, and it had belonged to a Second Class Petty Officer. It had the telltale "chevrons" on the sleeve. An officer walked by and glanced my way. He stopped, turned around, and said, "What rank are you, sailor?"

I told him that I was the Leading Seaman — a fact that he was thoroughly aware of. He was just looking for an excuse to bust my balls. This was the guy who hated my guts, and I related a story or two about this ass in the first volume in this series, *Urban Gothic*.

He went on to say, "What rank do I see represented on your sleeve?"

I replied, "Well, that would be a Second Class Petty Officer, Sir."

He reiterated my actual rank, and, so, I just reached over and tore the sleeve right off the shirt and threw it over the side. I said, "I have corrected the problem, Sir."

So I bought a brand-new pair of bell-bottom jeans — aka *blue denim work trousers* — and they were so stiff that you could stand them up in a corner and use them for spitball target practice. I ran into an old chief. These guys were generally like the Loveable Old Sergeants of Army lore — rough, gravel-voiced, hard-drinking guys. I approached the guy and said, "Hey, chief. I really hate new clothes. I had to replace my blue denim pants, and they are like sandpaper. What can I do to soften them up a little?" He told me what to do.

Onboard a ship, they have what is called a "Monkey Fist." It is a lightweight rope, about the size of a clothesline, with a steel ball embedded in fancy knot work on the end. These "Monkey Fists" were used for throwing a line. When you got close to the dock, you had to toss the "Monkey Fist" onto the pier and then tie up the big hawsers on the end so that the guys on the dock could pull them over and tie up the ship. You had to wet the rope so that it would fly through the air correctly.

One day, I had my "Monkey Fist" over the side, getting it good and wet. At the time, they were churning the propellers, trying to reposition the ship. Suddenly, the thing just started to whiz through my hands. It had gotten caught on the prop and was being rapidly wound around the shaft. I never told anyone about that little caper.

So the chief tells me to run the rope through every belt loop of the pants and throw them over the side, preferably off the fantail — or the back of the ship for you landlubbers. He said to let the pants just ride it out in the prop wash for a few hours and that that would soften them up nicely.

I did everything the chief told me to do except for the part about letting them ride the prop wash. You see, I threw them in the wash per se and forgot about them. Two days went by before I remembered my trousers out there in the Pacific Ocean, in the "fabric-softening stage." When I reeled them in, they were the size of Daisy Duke's shorts from *The Dukes of Hazzard* TV show. These pants had been reduced to little, itsy-bitsy cutoffs. I doubt if that same officer would have appreciated me wearing those skimpy things around the deck, chipping rust with my U.S. Navy standard-issue gonads exposed.

Catfish Cell Phone

My first cell phone was this gigantic black box they installed in the trunk of my Ford Thunderbird. It was 1990, and I'd started an advertising agency in Charleston, South Carolina, and needed extra communication ability. Relatively speaking, cell phones had come a long way by that time, and, of course, they've come a lot further with the passage of time.

This big black box occupied 15% of my trunk space. They ran wires all the way up to my console up front and bolted this big phone to the "hump" between the seats. *Rocket X, Calling Earth....* That's who I was — Rocketman.

I put a lot of mileage on that car and on that phone. To be quite honest, I would never have been able to operate a successful business without that thing in my car. As I roared down Interstate 25, I was on the phone talking about my next television commercial or other mysterious advertising-agency stuff.

That phone served me well, and when I sold the car, it went with it. By then, even in those few, short years, cell-phone technology had progressed by leaps and bounds. The newer units were more powerful and much smaller. That's why I let the dinosaur go when I traded the car.

1996 came along. I sold the business in Charleston and moved back to my hometown, Larksville, Pennsylvania. I made the mistake of promising my wife a dream house on the foundation of a rental property that I owned, and she called in the promise. So, I built her dream house for her — she helped and did quite well, I might add.

In the year 2000, I started another business, building design and property management.

Again, the business took off. I had four to five different projects going at any given time and started making money like crazy. So, to keep the momentum going, I contracted cell phones — two of them, to be exact. I had two lines with 5000 minutes per month per line, and still, I went over by the end of the month. That was when you bought minutes in a bundle and paid through the nose if you colored outside the lines. My cell-phone bill every month was obscene, but that's how business is done here in America.

I designed and built everything from custom kitchens and baths to entire houses. This was the nature of my business. In 2005, they started talking about revamping the entire building-code arrangement. The powers-that-be — the "International Building Code" people — decided to change *all* of the building codes, which meant that I would have to relearn *and* purchase all of the various code books and updates, a very expensive proposition.

With that looming over my head, I decided to pack it up in 2006. I retired. That was it — no more, I'm done, finished, hit the road, Jack, and don't you come back.

One day, not long after that momentous decision, I was driving down the road and just about to go over a bridge. I had my brand-new Motorola flip phone on the seat next to me. Under some sort of spell, I glanced in the rearview mirror and noticed there weren't any cars on the bridge. While in this trance, I pulled over to the railing, stopped the truck, grabbed my phone, and got out.

What happened in the next few seconds is legend. I hauled back and sailed that phone out over the Susquehanna River. *Kaplunk!*

Now, some big catfish is taking all my calls. That thing had turned into an electronic leash. It was liberating to do what I did — and, more importantly, I have not replaced that cell phone since.

The Mud Bath

My wife's kid sister is a real "slip" of a person.

What exactly does that mean? A "slip" of a person? I haven't the foggiest idea, but it seemed like the thing to say.

Getting on with it — her husband knocked her up (there's another one of those expressions that we don't really know the origin of), she was pregnant, and eventually gave birth to two identical twin boys. To this very day, I cannot tell them apart. When I attend a family function, I end up using slang nicknames like "Muscles" or "Handsome" — and then there's the always-useful "Ass Wipe" — but I think you get the picture.

Now, you must take into consideration the fact that I don't know anything about kids. I never had children. When I was getting my teaching certificate in Florida, it was suggested that I never — ever — consider a career in early-childhood development. This fact is very important to remember while you're reading this story.

The boys must have been around six or seven years old at the time. We had just finished building our house up in the mountains outside of a little town called Larksville. In fact, I still had a small bulldozer parked in the woods because I was working on a swale to divert the runoff water on the hill behind the house.

At that time, my sister-in-law had a real obsession with germs. We discussed this issue on more than one occasion. She had those little bottles of hand sanitizer just about everywhere: in her car, in her purse, on her person — you name it. There was always a jug of that goo hidden somewhere nearby.

So, they came to visit one day, and I was just sitting around doing nothing. It was Sunday, and that meant that I couldn't go and fire up my bulldozer to work on that swale. But I was itching to get at it. Something came up, and they — the sisters, that is — asked me to "babysit" the twins.

At first, I thought that they were joking. *Me? Babysit?* But, alas, they were dead serious. I had to watch the kids while they went down to the next town over to visit a thrift store. My wife and her sisters all do that — haunt thrift stores for the buy of a lifetime. Maybe they think a Ming Dynasty vase will appear on the shelves someday with a ridiculous $1 price tag on it. But, that unlikelihood notwithstanding, they do enjoy shopping at thrift stores.

But that left me alone with these two kids, whom I couldn't tell apart. It was like something out of an episode of *The Twilight Zone*. Hell, I had no clue what to do with two six- or seven-year-old boys. I don't play any sports that entail a ball. I'm not a "wood guy" who could show them how to build a Bat Cave out of one piece of wood. And I sure as hell can't impress them on a computer. First, I would have to figure out how to turn it on — and then it would all go downhill from there.

So, I get this bright idea. I had been sitting there chomping at the bit to go start my bulldozer. I would have jumped at any excuse — and here one was.

"Say, boys. Would you like to go for a bulldozer ride?"

Up into the woods we go. I fire up the old hurdy-gurdy and place them on either side of me. We go plowing up dirt between the trees while I work on my swale. It was pretty muddy, too, but that didn't stop Killdozer. We laugh at a little mud.

I made a few passes with the blade and pushed up a pile of dirt. I could see by the water running downhill that it was working; that's what I was looking for — drainage.

I stopped the machine and turned it off. I told the kids that that was it — end of the exciting bulldozer ride for that day. I lifted them down off the machine, jumped down myself, and proceeded to walk down through the woods toward the house, yelling over my shoulder as I went, "Come, kids — let's go and get a bologna sandwich."

I walked for a while and then realized that there wasn't any sound. Even though I'm ignorant when it comes to kids, I have enough presence of mind to know that, when they get real quiet, something is amiss.

When I turned around, there they were — rolling around in a huge mud puddle of my making. *Good God — how did that happen?*

I walk up and drag the two of them out of the puddle. They were both absolutely covered in fresh mud, and I freaked right the fuck out: *What do I do now?!*

I got them back to the house and made them strip down to their underpants. Then I threw their clothes into the washing machine. I washed and dried their clothes and got them redressed just as the sisters were returning from the thrift store.

It was a close call. I figured that, if their mother found out that her kids had been up to their asses in mud, she would have done a back flip on my face.

The moral of this story is simple: Don't give kids a ride on your bulldozer — under any circumstances.

Going Out in Manhattan

*L*isten, I can count on one hand the number of times I've gone to a dirty movie. One of those times is recounted in this book, in the story entitled "No Shave Zone."

Here is another misguided adventure involving viewing dirty pictures.

One day, my first wife's brother and I were just hanging out at their father's apartment on Park Avenue in New York. John's friend, from Temple University, was a guy named "Crotch." That was the only name I'd ever heard ascribed to this man — "Crotch" — and I haven't the foggiest idea, nor do I want to know, how he acquired that nickname.

It was February in Manhattan. If you have ever spent time in New York City, you know what that means. It gets colder than a wart on a witch's tit in New York City in the dead of winter.

So, we were there, just sitting around, doing nothing, when Crotch spoke up. He said that he'd never been to a dirty-picture show in his life. John and I just looked at one another. Hell, man, New York City is notorious for 42nd Street — dirty-picture joints as far as the eye can see in those few blocks.

We jumped into John's Saab automobile. First off, I was surprised that the damned thing started — but, then again, the Swedes have pretty cold winters, also. Now you have to imagine how we were dressed. We looked like hell. Back then, there wasn't anything called "Shabby Chic." We used The Salvation Army for our wardrobe out of necessity. We were starving college students. Each one of us had on a full-length overcoat with the collar turned up against the biting cold. John and Crotch were both wearing pulled-down watch caps, like the ones I used to wear in the Navy. We basically looked like a trio of bums, to be quite honest.

Anyway, we drove down from 72nd Street and Park Avenue to the 42nd Street area and sharked for a parking space. John parked his heap, and we walked around the corner to a dirty-picture place. This theatre had seen better days, maybe back in the 1940s some time. I do remember that we had to go up a flight of steps to get into the place. I think we were on 38th Street, but don't quote me on that — ask John or Crotch.

It was really cold that day, so, once we got in there, we took advantage of what little heat they provided. As it turned out, our questionable fashion was quite *en vogue* there. *Everyone* was wearing long overcoats and pulled-down watch caps. It must have been the preferred dress code of the dirty-picture crowd.

A few hours passed, and there were a number of films. The only one I remember was a piece called *Witches Brew Screw*. I'm serious — I'm not making that up. Well, as far as dirty pictures go, it was pretty well a standard suck-and-fuck story. Well, actually, there wasn't much of a *story*. I don't think anyone who patronizes these places does it for the fantastic dialogue or the rigorous Method School of Acting ability.

Finally, Crotch told us that he had seen enough, and we decided to leave.

Well, that's when it got interesting.

When we stepped outside into the cold, gray afternoon, unbeknownst to us, there was a street demonstration in progress against these "smut purveyors." There were about 50,000 people on the street carrying placards. Some pointed to us and started shouting, "There they are! There's some of them pigs now! Just look at them!"

We did manage to get out of there with our lives — but only by a c-hair.

I'm sure that Crotch will have something to tell his grandkids some day.

No-Shave Zone

*M*y wife is from a small city in northeastern Pennsylvania called Pittston.

This town is located equidistant between Wilkes-Barre and Scranton and enjoys a few distinctions. For example, it is the home of Rocky's Italian Butcher Shop, aka "Sabatelli's." (There is a story about Rocky's in the first book in this series, *Urban Gothic*.)

Pittston also has some really good pizza joints, and it also entertains members of the Mafia. They commute from there to New York and New Jersey, where they "work." I am not making this up. Go see for yourself. Just drive down the street; when you see a "Bathtub Madonna," you're probably very close.

If you aren't familiar with the "Bathtub Madonna" concept, I'll explain it to you: You take an old cast-iron bathtub and stand it up in your yard. You place it in a little hole or depression and then pour concrete all around it — and especially inside. Make a nice flat surface. Then go out and buy a statue of the BVM (Blessed Virgin Mary). Place shrubs all around, and presto! You have a Bathtub Madonna.

But that isn't what this story is about.

Another attribute that the city of Pittston used to have was a drive-in dirty-movie theatre. That is correct: a suck-and-fuck movie screen as big as Godzilla's backside, in an open-air environment. Don't ask me how they pulled that one off, but do refer to the part, above, about the Mafia living there.

This place was called "The Riverside Drive-In," and they screened dirty movies. Now, I wasn't really into that sort of thing, and I really don't have anything against it. I mean, if you're watching child porn, I may have a strong opinion about that, but people copulating on the big screen never really bothered me.

One night, a drinking buddy and I decided to go up to Pittston and actually pay to see a dirty movie. So, we grabbed a few six packs and plopped ourselves down at the Riverside Drive-In.

The movie that night was a film called *The Beaver Barber.* I kid you not. It was about this big guy who never said anything. He just grinned at these young, nubile girls and then did all kinds of things to their pubic region. He shaped the hair to look like a heart. One was done into a four-leaf clover, and another formed the word "Yes," detailed into the squiggly little hairs. Naturally, these haircuts had to be road-tested, so there were your standard-issue studly guys with very pronounced appendages working up a lather, with these young sweet things saying, "No. No. No," over and over again. I doubt if this film won any Academy Awards, but it did have an impact on me.

So, there I was, standing in my parents' bathroom — I still lived at home at the time; I think I was around 17 years old. I'm standing there at the bathroom sink, shaving, and the thought popped into my head: It had been months since I'd been to the Riverside Drive-In, but, all of a sudden, I got this uncontrollable urge to shave my pubic-hair area.

My rationale was simple: I would shave it like a large triangle and really impress the ladies. (I also thought that about a pair of shoes with "Cuban Heels." Do you remember those? This pair actually had these little red hearts on the inside, right under where the heel would rest. I thought they would appeal to the opposite sex, too, but I was sadly mistaken. I wish I could have remembered that when I was in the process of shaving my pubic hair.)

Well, nothing was going to divert me from this course of action, so I shaved the triangle into my pubic region. Little did I know at the time what kind of big mistake this was. It wasn't just a big mistake — it was a *huge* mistake.

At the time, I was driving one of my dad's tandem-axle dump trucks. "Tandem axle" simply means that it had a copious amount of rubber tires in the back where the load of coal rested. This job entailed getting loaded at the strip mine and hauling the coal to the "Breaker." That's where they processed the coal and beat it down into various sizes so it would fit into your stove or furnace.

Needless to say, I sat in a truck for eight solid hours a day, six days a week, going back and forth through the same small towns and up the same back roads, just hauling coal.

That's when the trouble started.

I really should have conferred with one of my lady friends prior to shaving my pubic hair. No one told me what happens when it starts to grow back. Where I shaved happens to rest right below my belt buckle.

I tried everything: Vaseline, axle grease — I even drove around all day with my pants undone. That would have been an interesting explanation if a cop had stopped me in my big truck:

"Son, why are you driving that huge truck with your knickers down around your knees?"

"Well, officer, it's like this: My friend and I decided to go see *The Beaver Barber* at the drive-in theatre in Pittston one night…"

Crazy but Not Stupid

*W*hen I was a kid, my brother and I would walk the mile down the dirt mountain road to the town of Larksville.

Our mom would give us a nickel apiece, and we would go down to Kelty's penny candy store. It was just a few doors away from the four-way stop at the bottom of the hill. Just to the left, on Luzerne Avenue, was a small service station and garage named "Jack's." Yes, that was it: "Jack's Garage."

Now, Jack's had a following of sorts — you could call them the "garage groupies." They were a bunch of old men who would hang out all day, surrounding the coal stove — a little "potbelly" stove positioned strategically in the middle of this room. These men would smoke cigars and solve the world's problems every day of the week and would tackle twice the usual number of issues on Saturday.

Larksville was a small town, and, as with any other small town, you had your basic assortment of characters. By "characters," I mean people with little quirks about them that everyone accepted as being unique to that particular individual.

There was one younger guy who was mentally challenged. Now, we didn't use that kind of terminology back in those days. I'm talking about the 1950s here — that's when I was a kid, in the 1950s. We would say something like "retarded," or "touched in the head." Some people used the word "slow" to describe this kind of person. Everyone knew about at least one mentally challenged person or knew someone who did. It wasn't any big deal. That was just life in a small town, and everyone accepted it.

But old men, smoking cigars and solving the world's problems do need a bit of humor every once in a while, so they would play a little trick on this guy, Donny. Every time Donny would go into Jack's, one of these elder statesmen would place a nickel and a dime on the glass case where Jack displayed his oil filters and spark plugs. They'd ask Donny to pick up one of the coins. Donny would always pick up the nickel and put it in his pocket. After he left, you could hear the howls of laughter coming from inside Jack's.

This went on for years — and I mean that literally: years. Larksville didn't change that much until I grew up. The candy got smaller in my hand, and the neat places in town were converted into welfare housing.

Finally one day, one of the elder statesmen asked Donny the critical question.

"You know, Donny, for years we've been playing this joke on you, and you always pick up the nickel. We have to know: why wouldn't you take the dime?"

Donny looked at the guy with a smile that only "slow" people have and said, "If I took the dime, you wouldn't play the trick on me anymore…"

With that, he turned and walked out.

I can assure you of one thing: On that particular day, no howls of laughter were to be heard.

Being Weightless

My book *Urban Gothic* was dedicated to my older brother, Bill.

He died at 61 years of age — far too young for such an interesting man. Bill was unusual. All of his life, he wrestled with a weight issue. He tried "Weight Watchers" and some of those other diet plans where they send you boxes of food every week. He tried hypnosis. He even tried Transcendental Meditation.

Finally, he was able to bring his weight under control.

But then he went and became a gourmet chef! This guy would take the current food magazines and replicate a meal — right down to the particular garnish. It would come out looking like the photograph and probably tasted even better.

All of us brothers were into speed. If a lawnmower bogged down in the grass, we would yank the engine, bore it out, put a racing camshaft into it, and up the horsepower. That's the way it was for us — everything had to be fast.

Bill bought a cherry 1963 Corvette. It was a beautiful car — red and white, a nice 283 cubic-inch engine, with a four-speed. I drove it. The car was nice.

The engine started to smoke a little. That was an issue that plagued the early Chevy 283 ci engines. They burned oil — a lot of oil. So my brother pulled out the engine, bought a 327 motor, and sent it down to Georgia to have it balanced and blueprinted. What this means is that you could rev the engine to extremely high RPMs without blowing the thing through the hood.

The engine was taken apart, and all of the tolerances were re-worked so that it was spot-on. Let me put it this way: when the motor was finished, it had 534 horsepower! By today's standards, that doesn't sound like much. But, I can assure you, back in the 1960s and 1970s, that was just incredible, especially if you dropped it into a lightweight 1963 Corvette. That car just screamed. I drove it twice, and when you put your foot into it, the force would drive your body back into the seat — it was that fast.

Well, Bill street-raced it and cleaned everyone's clock. Then he got bored. He told me it wasn't fast enough for him. Bill was like that. He wouldn't blab about what he was doing — he just did it, without saying a word.

One day, he announced that he'd sold the Corvette and bought an airplane. *Wait a minute, Bill. Flying a plane is a lot different from slamming gears in a fast, souped-up car!*

He went out and bought a Piper "Cub." It was small and slow, but it was the airplane he cut his flying teeth on. Years passed, and Bill continued to study the subject of flying. He would go down to Opa-locka, Florida, a place outside of Miami, and study flying. He did that for years and was awarded every rating there was — twin engine, jet engine, helicopter, glider — hell, he was even checked off on balloons.

In the meantime, he bought a nice Cessna 165. It was a great plane. It cruised at 165 mph, had a good range, and was just a nice plane to fly. In order to keep up his hours for his flying license, he would go up every weekend and ask any of us if we wanted to go with him. He and I did this many times. We would jump in the plane and fly down to Allentown just for a cheeseburger, and then fly back to Wilkes-

Barre. On one of those flights, he told me this
story.

Bill kept his plane at a small airport in Forty
Fort, Pennsylvania. To offset his rent payments,
he would fly "Scenic Flights" on the weekends
in a twin-engine Beechcraft. This also gave him
the hours that he needed for his pilot's license.

On one of our little excursions in his plane,
he showed me this technique where he would
just push the stick forward and drop the plane
about 1,000 feet in a matter of seconds. Two
things would happen: The first was that your
stomach ended up in your mouth, and the
second was the sensation of weightlessness.
The astronauts use a plane they call the
"Vomit Comet" to do the same thing when
they train. It's a specially outfitted jetliner that
flies elliptical circles and gives its occupants
weightless conditions for a number of seconds
at a time.

Anyway, Bill was flying these "Scenic Flights"
when, one day, two gay guys came aboard
his plane. He told me that he would ask his
passengers if one of them wanted to sit up
front in the right-hand seat, a position in the
airplane that, normally, people would fight
over. But, on this day, neither of his passengers
was interested. He took them up, and they

huddled in the back seat. He'd fly around, and they'd have him do this dive a few times, and that would be it. Bill said they always tipped him on top of the cost of the flight and walked away smiling. Every month, the same two guys would show up and ask my brother to take them up.

Bill told me that he never even peeked. He said he really didn't want to know what was going on in the back seat. But on the bright side, he never had to clean up after them, either.

The Safety Razor

*D*o you remember the "Dickie"?
It was a piece of men's apparel that came out in the late 1960s and early 1970s. This item of menswear redefined the term "mock turtleneck." It was a regular turtleneck collar, with two pieces of the same fabric, which you tucked into a standard dress shirt. The thing was rather ridiculous, because it would bunch up under your shirt and form a noticeable bump in either the back or the front.

Well, I owned a few of these, along with the light-blue, double-breasted blazer. That was standard cocktail lounge menswear in those days. If you didn't don your "Dickie," then you could choose an ascot with the matching breast-pocket handkerchief. This thing was strictly for show. It was made out of rayon or some other man-made fabric that was slippery — it wouldn't wipe anything off if there was an accident or something.

So when I returned from Vietnam, it was
1970. About the only thing that I retained
from my official government-issue sea bag and
uniform were the little kits. They gave us a
shaving kit and a little sewing kit, which I had
for years. The shaving kit came with a "safety"
razor. Why it was called a "safety razor" is
anyone's guess, because there was nothing "safe"
about this device. It was based on a design from
the Medieval period, purportedly developed
by the Marquis de Sade in collaboration with
Monsieur Guillotine.

The only "safe" feature of this face rapier was
the loading system. On the bottom of the razor
was a little knob that you turned to open the
two trapdoors on the top. If you turned the
razor over and worked with this system, it
looked just like the bomb-bay doors of a Flying
Fortress. *(Note: At this juncture, the reader should
make airplane sounds and whistle, like bombs being
dropped. This will add spice to this otherwise very
boring story.)*

Well, you turned the knob, opened the top
doors, and slid a double-edged razor blade into
this suicide device. The thing was quite clunky;
it wasn't balanced, because it had all that weight
on top. So, when you shaved with it, the thing
was hard to control. Nothing like the razors we

use today, with the twin and triple blades.

When you shaved with the "Double-Edged Safety Razor," you planned on getting cut. Before starting, you would dig out your styptic pencil and make little wads out of toilet tissue. You may remember that — rolling up a small piece of toilet tissue and sticking it on your shaving cuts to stem the flow of blood. This would have made a great psychological torture device. Give the inmate a Double-Edged Safety Razor and no styptic pencil. In fact, take away the toilet tissue, too — that would be so cruel.

Well, I'm in my parents' only bathroom. Back then, most houses had only one bathroom. It wasn't like today, when every bedroom is *en suite*. You had to wait your turn. Naturally, my dad went first, primarily because it was *his* bathroom to begin with, and he would not fail to remind you of that fact on a daily basis. That meant he could take as long as he wished, and you just had to eat it — date or no date.

Yo, dad. Are you finished yet?

Watch your step, boy. I could be in here for hours if you aren't very careful.

OK. Thanks, dad. I'll just go wash up in the creek.

Finally, my turn would come. I showered and did my hair. Then I pulled out the dreaded "Double-Edged Safety Razor."

With trembling fingers, I loaded a brand-new blade into the hopper on top and carefully turned the knob to close the bomb-bay doors. I was ready to begin the massacre.

On this particular evening, I was let off easily. I had only six cuts on my face, as opposed to the usual eight — with one of them near fatal. However, the styptic pencil wasn't doing the trick to stem the flow of my precious Type O blood, and, so, I had to resort to the toilet-paper trick.

Now, keep in mind that the "Dickie" wasn't the full turtleneck; in fact, it was far from it. So, when I finished in the bathroom, I went and got dressed. By this time, someone else was using the bathroom, so I just decided to head downtown, as it was getting late.

On that night, I was going to hang out at my favorite cocktail lounge — "Vispi's." It was a really nice place that was owned by a gay guy, and, for that reason, it attracted a lot of chicks, because women are not threatened by homosexual men. But I was the shark in the swimming pool that night.

Here I am, 20 years old and studly as hell, 100% pure beef, American male. Recently discharged from the Navy, I was in the best shape of my life, a god just waiting to mate with a mere mortal.

I walked up to the bar and asked Leo, my favorite bartender, for my usual — a Black Russian. I spied two attractive young things across the bar, so I told Leo to fix them up with whatever they were drinking. We smiled back and forth and made those little one-finger, pinky-finger waves sort of things.

Everything was going just fine. I was in top form — a really well-rehearsed chauvinist pig, when the time came to head to the men's room. So, with genuine flourish, I motioned to Leo to refill my glass by swirling my index finger around above it and gave a small salute, indicating that I would return shortly.

I walked into the men's room, and, as I passed the sink area, naturally, I just had to look at myself. There in the mirror, staring blatantly back at me, was my face — with six tiny, blood-soaked wads of toilet tissue strategically stuck on various areas about my cheeks and neck. It was just mortifying. How the hell could Hugh Hefner's protégé step back into the lounge area after that performance?

As I slipped out the back door — which meant that I would have to walk completely around the strip mall because my car was in front of the place — I wondered why Leo didn't say anything to me.

Then it dawned on me: He knew that I was an artist and may have figured that I was doing this on purpose — some form of performance art.

On that occasion, my own, carefully constructed public image failed me entirely. I had to wait months before returning to Vispi's Cocktail Lounge.

Having a Bad Day

*A*s you may know, all of my stories are factual.

These things actually did occur — and, usually, exactly the way I describe them. Granted, I may change the names of people or businesses involved, but that's only in the interest of avoiding any major legal action.

But, allow me to share this next story with you. I cut this article out of the newspaper and carried it with me for years. Whenever someone would say that they were "…having a bad day," I would pull out the article and show it to them. In fact, that was the actual title of the article: "You Think You Had a Bad Day."

This incident took place in Gainesville, Florida, with the article originally appearing in the *West Palm Beach Post,* a newspaper that I subscribed to for many years while living in south Florida.

A friend stopped by his buddy's house to show him his brand-new motorcycle. They were behind the house, near the patio area. The first guy sat on the bike and was playing with the handlebars when he accidentally hit the electric "Start" button. The bike came to life and took off, with him on it. It crashed through his sliding glass doors, and he ended up in the living room of his house. An ambulance was called, and he was taken to the emergency room and patched up for minor cuts and abrasions.

Meanwhile, the gasoline had run out of the bike's gas tank onto the floor, and the guy's wife sopped it up with a rag and wrung it out in the guest-bathroom toilet.

The owner of the house came back and decided to use the bathroom. He actually went in there with a lit cigarette, and, when he finished it, he threw it in the toilet. The problem was that he was still sitting on the thing. It exploded and burned him in areas of his anatomy that the stuff of nightmares are made of.

Again, they called an ambulance. They came out to the house and loaded the poor guy up and proceeded to transport him to the hospital. But, on the way, while driving at breakneck speed, they got into a major wreck, and the guy ended up with both of his legs being broken.

Anytime I think that I'm having a bad day, my thoughts always go back to that little article I cut out of the newspaper.

Mistaken Identity

*I*f you were anywhere near northeastern Pennsylvania in the early 1970s, you would have heard about The Great Flood.

It was called "The Agnes Flood," and it put the word "inundated" into the mouths of everyone who lived there, a word whose definition no one knew prior to this event.

It was 1972. I was lying on the beach in Palm Beach, Florida. I lived in a condo there with my first wife, who just happened to have come from Big Money out on Long Island. There I was, just working on my tan and listening to the ocean lap the sand, when one of my neighbors came over to me. This old guy and I used to chat occasionally while doing our laundry. He must have retained some of that conversational information, because he walked up and said, "You're from that coal-cracking region up in Pennsylvania, aren't you?"

I answered in the affirmative to that.

Then he shoved a copy of *The Miami Herald* in my face and said, "Well, look at this."

There they were, the two concrete eagles that graced the tops of the pillars of the Market Street Bridge, sticking up out of this vast stream of muddy water.

I lost my breath and said, "When the hell did this happen?"

Well, it was obvious to the old guy that all of that kind of information would be provided in the article, so he just walked away, shaking his head.

Young whippersnappers. Think they know everything.

I went ahead and filed for a sabbatical from the university and then booked a flight up to Wilkes-Barre. After landing in New York, I took the bus for the four-hour ride up there. When the bus arrived in Wilkes-Barre, it had to go to a makeshift station at the K-Mart on the east side of the river. Their regular bus station was under 30 feet of water, which had flooded the town about three days before I arrived.

This presented a problem for me. I lived on the other side of the river, about five miles away, and I had to get over there. They told me that there was no way I was going to get across anytime soon, because *all* of the bridges

— except one — were out or disabled. So, I grabbed my duffle and started walking, not knowing exactly what I was going to do at the time.

As I walked, a large Army truck wheeled up and stopped alongside of me. It turned out that the driver was Jake, a guy I knew who was in the Army Reserve.

He said, "Jump in the back and cover yourself with that tarp. I'll get you over to the other side." It was like paying Charon to ferry you across the River Styx — the visuals were just as hellish.

I saw some of the worst devastation that I'd ever seen to that date, and — trust me — I'd seen some pretty heavy destruction in Vietnam, so I knew what I was talking about. There was only one bridge being used, and it was for "authorized personnel" only. Don't you just love that? *"Authorized Personnel" Only!* What exactly does that mean during a major destructive event like this? More than 400,000 people had been directly affected by this flood, and only two had flood insurance.

Entire blocks of houses had ceased to exist. I saw holes where homes used to be, and the smell was overpowering — a mixture of diesel fuel, rotten vegetables, shit, and death.

On the other side of the Carey Avenue Bridge, Jake stopped and yelled back, "Here's where you get off. I have to go down Route 11. Jump out here." Which I did — and thanked him profusely for the lift.

I proceeded to walk and hitchhike up to Larksville Mountain, where my parents' house was located.

I grew up in the heavy-equipment and trucking industry. That's what my father's business was all about. If there ever was a time for us to help bail out the rest of Wyoming Valley, this surely was it. Our garages and yard were located on high ground, so we were not affected at all. This allowed us to go right to work.

We went through some of the small towns on the west side, cleaning up the streets. They told everyone to throw everything out into the street, and it was our task to load this stuff up and haul it to a dump. When I say "everything," I mean just that — *everything*.

Allow me to get to the point of this story. After a few months, when things started to settle down into some semblance of normalcy, we were doing a lot of demolition work around the town of Plymouth. We would go in and weaken the house with chainsaws and then wrap a cable around it and pull the thing with a bulldozer.

This would crush the house, and we would haul it away. After doing this a few times, we all got pretty good at it.

There was another company called "Connelly & Son," who, you could say, was our competition. Not that it made any difference — there was plenty of work to go around. But, one day, their crew showed up at a house. They smashed the thing into the ground, loaded everything out, and brought in some dirt to fill the hole. After six hours, the only thing left was a vacant lot with a circle of fresh dirt in the middle.

Here is where the problem came in.

They had the right address as far as the address number was concerned. The problem was that they were on the wrong street.

This young couple came home from work to find that their entire house, complete with all their possessions, was simply gone. They were greeted by an empty lot.

I'm not sure if GPS would have corrected this little oversight or not. But, in 1972, no one could have dreamed of technology in that category. Then again, 'dozer jocks and truck drivers are not noted for being the sharpest pencils in the box when it comes to following directions.

Cold Beer Duct

For a while, I served on an LST in Vietnam with the Navy. While the official name of the vessel was "Landing Ship Transport," they were better known by their crews as "Long, Slow Targets." The ships were used in World War Two to transport Army tanks up onto the beaches of wherever they were needed. The boat had a giant anchor on the back and a big hold that could carry of bunch of Sherman tanks or whatever it was that you wanted placed on the beach. The objective was to drop the stern anchor as you steamed in and then use it to winch yourself off the sand when the transfer was complete.

Onboard, I served as a Boatswain's Mate. We did anything that concerned the upper decks and superstructure. We were known as "Deck Apes" because we were usually well muscled and very tan, especially while serving in Vietnam.

One day, a Chief Petty Officer asked me to join him while he repaired different things below decks. I was nothing more than his "gofer" and carried his toolbox for him. We went into the NCO ("Non-commissioned Officer") living quarters. These were the other guys who ran the ship; the dudes with the scrambled eggs on their hats were upstairs.

Allow me to explain this little gem of Navy terminology: "Scrambled eggs" refers to the gold-thread embroidery on the peak of the officers' caps. The more of this stuff, the higher up the food chain the officer was. It consisted of anchors, eagles, guys walking the plank, men swabbing decks — that sort of thing. But don't ask me where the terms came from because I can't tell you.

But I can explain an "NCO" — "Non-commissioned Officer." If I'm not mistaken, anything above an Ensign in the Navy was a Non-commissioned Officer. Most NCOs were in the E-1 to E-8 pay grade, otherwise known as abject poverty in the armed forces. You would be amazed by what we pay people who go out and risk their lives on our behalf — practically peanuts.

It seemed that the NCOs' air-conditioner wasn't working too well. I couldn't find any pity or empathy in my soul, because I slept in the stern division, and we didn't have any air-conditioning at all. So, *Boo-Hoo!* to these guys.

The old chief pulled apart the A/C unit and started to check all of the controls. He hooked up his gauges and checked to see if the compressor was working properly — which it was. He stood there, scratching his head. "I don't understand this. Everything checks out perfectly." So, he decided that there must be a blockage in the ductwork overhead.

"Hand me that Phillip's Head. I have to take this ductwork apart and check it out. So, I complied, and he unscrewed the clamps and started wrestling with the ductwork. It suddenly popped open, and all of these cans of beer — Hamm's Beer, to be exact — came rolling out, thumping him in the chest. It was ridiculous. These cans of cold beer just kept coming — there must have been a case stuffed in there. It sounded like a big ape beating his chest — *Thump! Thump! Thump!* They just kept on coming.

The chief told me to go get a bag of some kind, pick up all this beer, and take it to his cabin. He told me he was going to "…fix this problem for good…."

He disabled the entire air-conditioning unit

and said, "There! Let's see if that doesn't put an end to this!" You must understand that this was a very harsh form of punishment. In Vietnam, during the afternoon, you couldn't rest your hand on the inside of the bulkhead because of the heat. It would reach 95 degrees every day — not to mention the humidity, which air conditioning, of course, takes out of the sir. In essence, these guys were fucked. They should have had enough sense not to complain about their A/C unit in the first place.

Saigon Haircut

*M*ost of my time spent in Vietnam was on the Mekong River.

We would cruise up that river all the way to Cambodia. This caused problems for me later on. When I went to get college credits — the main reason I'd enlisted in the Navy to begin with — I was denied four times.

Later in life, I found out why. As it turned out, my official records had been whitewashed, because being in Cambodia in 1970 was considered to be Black Operations. President Nixon was on television, telling the world that we were not in Cambodia, and I was there practically every other week.

It required more than 35 years and three letters from a few of the officers I'd served under to get benefits, but that isn't what this story is about, now — is it?

During those bi-weekly periods, we would spend about three days in Saigon or Vung Tau.

The reason for this was confidential, and I am not at liberty to discuss it, but it doesn't matter, anyway.

One afternoon, an officer told me that my hair was getting too long and that I should have it cut prior to returning to my boat. He made it clear that this wasn't necessarily a request. So, before I started my drinking exercise on Tudo Street, I decided that I'd better take care of this business first.

I walked into a small "barbershop" and sat in the chair. The guy had it right in the front window because it was his pride and joy. Just having a real, live barber chair was reason enough to advertise it. So, there I was, having my hair cut. He spoke English, and he asked me if I wanted a manicure, and I said, "Fine." Then he asked about a massage of my shoulders and chest, so I agreed to that, too. There I was, sitting in this window in Saigon, having my hair cut and getting a manicure and a massage, all at the same time.

When he asked me if I would care for a blow job, that's when I decided to decline the guy's offer.

The way I saw it, that was entirely too much detail to expose in the window of this barbershop in Vietnam.

Your Papers, Please

I don't know what it is with these foreign customs people, but it seems they see me coming and decide to make my life more confusing than it already is.

This time, we had taken the overnight ferry from Portland, Maine, to Halifax, Nova Scotia. It was a pleasant trip. We did a little gambling and ate some bad seafood, but, all in all, it was nothing that we couldn't handle.

I'd rented a Mustang convertible in advance. When we were about three miles out from the harbor in Nova Scotia, I could see this bright-yellow blob on the pier. I turned to my wife and said, "I'll wager that is our Mustang." Sure enough, it was the car, a bright-yellow car, the only bright-yellow automobile in Nova Scotia.

Anyway, the thing that disembarked you at the pier was broken. They said that the damage had just then occurred, but I was not convinced. This thing was so covered in rust that it was orange — it hadn't worked in years. That meant that we had to queue up on the pier with our bags, in a long line reminiscent of the food lines you might see in Mogadishu.

After what seemed hours, we entered the Customs Building. I got in front of the desk, and the guy seated there looked up and said the following: "How do you intend to protect yourself while staying here in Nova Scotia?"

I paused, looked at him, and said, "Excuse me?"

He asked me again, "How do you intend to protect yourself while here in Nova Scotia?"

I asked him if there was something I really need to know about, like rabid bears, or a flock of serial killers. *Please explain this to me. Maybe I can get the next ship out of here.*

After we got situated in our bright-yellow Mustang, I had a chance to reflect upon the guy's question. My only answer was that he was trying to lure me into whipping out my hidden stash of assault weapons — like a Colt .45, a model 1918, a giant bowie knife, or something like that.

Man, those Canadian Customs officials are a sneaky lot — I'll grant you that.

Rocco's Bar

*T*he area around Wilkes-Barre, Pennsylvania, is dotted with small communities that were given life by a ruthless coal industry. Many men labored daily in the bowels of the earth extracting that black scourge, making a few rich and ruining the workers' lungs in the process.

Because of this dust, the miners needed to clear their throats with cold beer prior to returning home after a long shift in the mines. This fact gave rise to what are commonly called "gin mills" or, simply, "beer gardens." I haven't a clue where the idea of a "garden" came from. These places were basically dives, even on a good day. They were the kind of barroom that stuck your elbows to the bar as soon as you laid them down, and served skunky beer and pickled pigs' feet, kept cold on top of the bar, where the cooler rested. Rocco's bar started out as one of these places and evolved into a neighborhood establishment after the demise of the below-ground coal industry back in the 1960s.

The first time I had any dealings with Tony at Rocco's was back in the '70s. I had a girl in my MGB convertible and was making my way over the mountain for an afternoon picnic of sorts. Naturally, in order to try to guarantee any success in the romance department, I packed a bohemian lunch of bread, cheese, and wine. The problem was that I didn't have a wine opener, or "corkscrew," as it is commonly called. While driving up Wilson Street in the little town of Larksville, I spied Rocco's Bar and decided to wheel in and have my wine cork removed. I told my date that I would be right back.

I went up the steps and entered the dark, cool environment of a gin mill in summer. Tony was behind the bar, and his brothers, who I came to know, eventually, were on the stools opposite. They were all drinking draught beers. I walked in and asked if they could pop the cork from my bottle of wine.

"Sure — we can do that."

So, Tony digs around behind the bar and comes up with a corkscrew. He opens the bottle and starts admiring the label. "This looks like a very fine wine. I would bet that it's some kind of vintage."

Then he put the bottle to his lips and chugged a mouthful. Then he passed the bottle to his brothers, who, in turn, chugged on the bottle until it was gone. Bob handed me the empty bottle, and they all thanked me.

I said, "Hey! You guys drank all of my wine!"

They said, "Wow! That's very observant of you. You must be a man of fine detail. Yes, we did, and it was quite good, I might add."

They all returned to their beers and conversation and just ignored me. I ended up standing there, feeling like a foolish person, wondering how I was going to handle this situation. Finally, I decided that I should just leave and deal with this another time. As I exited the place, Tony threw the cork at me, adding insult to injury.

Some time passed, and my brother asked me to meet him for a cold one after work. I said, "Sure. Where?"

He mentioned this place called Rocco's Bar. I told him about my experience there, and he assured me that that was typical Rocco brothers behavior and that they didn't mean anything by it. That was just the way they were. As time went on, I eventually learned how true that statement was.

My art studio was located in Larksville, the same town Rocco's Bar was in. In fact, the place was only a few blocks up the street from my location, so I decided that it was safer to just walk up there instead of driving, especially when I knew I would be a bit tipsy upon my return.

One week, an old girlfriend of mine flew into town to visit me. She was a native of Boulder, Colorado, and I'd met her out there while operating heavy equipment for Boulder Excavators. We'd had a vibrant sex life for the few months that our little tryst had lasted, and, so, I guessed that she was interested in sampling more of the same. So she came to Larksville and stayed at the infamous Alchemy Studio.

One night, we were just lying around, and I suggested that we walk up to Rocco's for a few pops, and she agreed.

As soon as we were situated at the bar, I knew this evening was going to take a turn south. When asked where she was from, Cheryl responded in a hoity-toity voice, "I am from Boulder."

You see, she didn't realize that these guys were not simple country bumpkins — they got around. She just assumed that they were hicks and that she was from some far-superior place. That didn't go over too well with the boys.

Tony looked at her and asked, "Is that anywhere near Little Rock?"

The place went nuts.

Then Bob noticed her leather boots and commented on them.

"Boy, those are some fine-looking boots you have there."

"Yes, they are. These boots are Frye boots."

Tony said, "Golly. I've never seen a Frye boot. Would you mind showing them to me?"

So, Cheryl took off one of her Frye boots and handed it to Tony. I was sitting there thinking, *Nothing good can come out of this.*

Tony acted like he was admiring this boot, turning it this way and that, when, suddenly, he shoved the boot under the beer tap — I think it was Rolling Rock. Then he proceeded to fill the boot with beer.

After it was full, Tony took a long pull of beer from Cheryl's boot. Then he passed it to me, and everyone had to drink beer from this Frye boot. But again, to add insult to injury, when the boot got to Cheryl, Tony grabbed it and said, "Nope. Woman drink last from the Holy Boot!"

Up until that point, Cheryl was laughing and playing along. Then she got pissed — she was a self-styled Women's Libber at the time.

All I remember is the walk back to Alchemy Studio.

Every other step went *Squish! Squish! Squish!*

Alternative Pre-Op

*D*uring the mid-1980s, running all the way into 2003, I underwent eight lower-back surgeries.

Some of the damage was from Vietnam, and some came from an industrial accident in Key West, Florida. Four of these surgeries were done at CMC Hospital in Scranton, Pennsylvania, under the careful eye of Doctor Black, a local neurosurgeon of good standing in the area commonly called northeastern Pennsylvania.

I don't know if you are familiar with the protocol following a major surgical procedure for the back. You are not allowed to go into the shower for several days — at least that's the way it used to be. I haven't had the need to be sliced and diced for several years.

The evening before my third surgery, I had my wife find a barber to come into the hospital and cut my hair. There is nothing worse than having long, greasy hair for days on end after a surgery, and, trust me, that powdered shampoo they give you isn't worth a tinker's damn (whatever *that* means — I just wanted to use the expression somewhere in this text).

Teresa found a guy, all right. He was a hair stylist and agreed to come in that evening to shorten my locks. It wouldn't have been half bad if this guy was some Italian dude with a coiffured hairdo of his own, but, as it turned out, the guy was really, really gay.

So, there was Maurice, dancing around my head with a pair of scissors and commenting on the quality of my hair — *and* the quantity, I might add — when Doctor Black came walking into the room. In my limited vision, I did not consider it necessary to confer with the good doctor prior to making these arrangements.

He wasn't too pleased.

Doctor Black considered himself to be quite the ladies' man, and I gather that, when you go probing into other people's brains, you could easily construct an image of yourself as being a vanguard of sorts. When he realized that my Maurice was very, very gay, his facial expression spoke volumes on the subject.

In my own defense, I explained to Doctor Black what it was like going for days without a shower — let alone the tangled mess sitting on top of my head. He seemed to warm to the logic of this endeavor. I must admit that my guy's attitude didn't help matters at all. Maurice seemed to become even more animated, giving a nonstop dissertation on the travails of being a hair stylist in the modern world — which just poured more adjectives into my doctor's opinion of the man — or woman, depending upon the way one would view this episode.

Maurice finally completed his task, a handful of my hard-earned cash changed hands, and a pile of hair was strewn about my chair.

Doctor Black was good enough to send Housekeeping up to clean the place after all was said and done.

Hotel Comrade

*B*ack in 1989, I took my wife on a trip around the whole of Europe.

We traveled by train and made a loop from Cherbourg, France, up the coast to Amsterdam, and then over into what at that time were the communist countries. One of our stops was in Budapest, and it was quite memorable, to say the least.

When we arrived, it was necessary to go through Customs. Being that we were traveling quite light, I had my shaving kit in my carry bag. The Customs officers were doing their jobs, digging through my stuff, when suddenly this little fat guy stopped and jumped back. Then he summoned his associates over, and all five of them gathered around my shaving kit. The grabbed for their guns and started to undo the little snaps on the holsters.

Finally, the original little fat guy handed me my kit and pointed. He wanted me to extract an item from its recesses, and I figured out what it was. I reached in and pulled out my switchblade, held it up, and flicked the button.

Out snapped my moustache comb.

What was funny was how these guys jumped back when the "blade" snapped out. Now that I think about it, that would have been a good way to get shot, right there at the Customs counter.

After that little international incident was clarified, we moved on with our plans to stay in Budapest. At the information kiosk, some money changed hands, and we were whisked away in a Mercedes taxicab to a private apartment. This was what the bribe was about — this guy's chance to rent us his apartment for the night, complete with a bathtub in the kitchen.

I went nuts. The only word I knew in Russian came from my friend Nikita Krushchev banging his shoe at the United Nations and swearing that he would bury me, all the while screaming out *Nyet! Nyet!* over and over again. *Nyet* means "No."

I grabbed our bags and beat a hasty retreat from this apartment block in downtown Budapest. We walked aimlessly through all of the drunken people — this was the very night that Hungary finally became free of their Russian handlers. Everyone was plastered and singing in the streets. *Hooray for Freedom,* I suppose.

I finally stumbled upon a hotel. This place was really a piece of work, one of the finer examples of Russian architecture, complete with corridor floors that had hills in them. I am not making this up. The floors were actually waving at us. My thought was that this place could collapse into a pile of masonry at any minute.

Allow me to give you a little travel tip, especially if you are traveling in the former USSR: take a pocketful of Kennedy half-dollars with you. They will open doors — literally. For some odd reason, JFK is a real hero over there. I tipped our porter with one of these. At first he looked at it with a touch of disgust on his face, thinking that I had just stiffed him — until he realized that the coin had Kennedy on its face. Or should I say that Kennedy's face was on the coin. I could do no wrong after that. We were truly comrades.

He opened our room with great flourish and revealed a small closet with a huge television set. The TV was so big that you had to climb on the bed to get around it. When we turned it on, there was only one channel — MTV, with

some Russian chicks jumping around singing in
a guttural language and saying something about
babushkas and babies.

The bathroom was even more thrilling. The
shower curtain was about eight inches short,
so when you were taking a shower (in cold
water), all of the excess water came streaming
out onto the floor. The toilet-paper holder was
something right out of the tractor factory. It was
made from heavy-gauge iron — you could use
this to pull an engine from an automobile or
your neighborhood T-34 tank.

After that enlightenment, we moved on to
the room service. I called down to the front
desk and went through four people trying
to overcome the language barrier. I finally
convinced them that we were starving and
needed some nourishment. The same porter/
bellboy came up about an hour later with
this huge tray, on which had been placed: a
big hunk of bread, one length of sausage, two
pickles, and a block of cheese. There wasn't
any silverware or knives. I guess they'd heard
about my encounter at the Customs office and
decided to err on the side of good judgment
by not giving me a knife. I may have wanted
to commit *hari kari* in the room — you never
know.

The next morning, we'd had enough of Budapest and decided to leave. I had to convert some of my greenbacks into a wad of money, the local currency. At the train station, I handed Teresa this big wad of notes and told her to go spend them on something. She came back empty-handed. She said that the shops would take only American or German currency — dollars or *marks*.

Hours later, we rolled into Italy. I went to the money exchange and pushed this tangle of bills under the little window. The guy shoved it back. I then pushed it further into his domain, and, again, he pushed it back, with this piece of wisdom: "How do you say — 'paper your walls….."

I still have some of those goulash bills in my "man" box.

Closing the Incision

*M*ajor back surgery is not for the faint-hearted.

There is an old saying somewhere in the annals of medicine that states "…one back surgery is too many…."

I never had the chance to heed that sage advice, especially after Number Eight was performed on the L-4, L-5 region of my back. Many of these procedures were performed at CMC Hospital in Scranton, Pennsylvania, covering a period of several years. I'd been severely injured in Vietnam and then again in Key West, Florida after a major industrial accident.

One thing about multiple back surgeries is the fact that the percentages start running against you. The night before this operation, each member of the Operating Room team comes to see you and explain what is going to happen to your body the following morning. The anesthesiologists will tell you about the 'Caine family of drugs that they intend to inject into your flesh. The surgeon will stop by to scare the crap out of you with his predictions of what could go wrong.

"Well, Mr. Goodman, there is a 30% chance that you will never walk again and a 50% chance that you will never have a normal bowel movement for the rest of your life. Oh! Did I mention the fact that you may never use your penis again for anything other than spontaneous urination?"

They go on and on. Even your ancestors are affected. "We have a 40% chance that you will never see your loved ones in Valhalla, but you may text them from purgatory — with permission, of course."

So, while your "gelatin jewels" slowly melt on your dinner tray, this stream of foreboding continues way past the movie you were looking forward to watching all day. All that this accomplishes is that you're not able to sleep for the next six years worrying about the total collapse of your body as you have known it.

The big day arrives, and you get wheeled down into the bowels of the hospital. They always roll you past the morgue — just for effect. Then a guy with a round mirror on his head starts telling you about his golf game, and you notice the telltale effects of too many martinis manifesting themselves in the hand shaking he exhibits.

The operating room is always freezing after the nurse strips off your gown, which isn't any big loss, seeing that your ass was exposed to everyone who cared to look — and then the nurse offers you a sheet. They strap you to the table and extend your arms so that needles can be inserted without a lot of trouble. Finally, that fateful command comes: "I want you to start counting backwards from 100."

"99, 98, 97, 96, 95," — welcome to la-la land, bucko!

Afterwards, you *sort of* wake up in a strange environment. The first thing that has to be done is ripping out the catheter in your manhood — that thing has to go! But the PAC nurses see it another way. They don't have a penis, so they can't appreciate the finer attributes of having a plastic pipe stuck up in your dick.

Finally, after an hour or so, you return to the land of the make-believe people, groggy and disoriented, but intact — for the most part.

At the time, I didn't know that they had installed the pads for a TENS unit right in the Operating Room. The thing was cranked up to its maximum output when Nurse Axe decided to change the dressings. All I heard was a loud *Thump!* as her body impacted the wall next to my bed. I apologized profusely and claimed ignorance, but it didn't matter. I had just made an enemy for life.

After several days — 12, to be exact — I was summoned into the hospital for the ritual of having the staples removed. Because I'd had so many surgeries in the same place, I'd suggested that they use Velcro back there to close the thing up. That way, it would be easier to go back in at any time. The-powers-that-be didn't see it that way and decided to use staples instead — and a lot of staples were used, indeed. The nurse counted them and announced that there were 78 of these little metal bastards in my back.

Then she started laughing. I won't say it was an hysterical laugh, but it was more than just a belly laugh. Because these staples were in my back, I couldn't see what all this mirth was about, and I started to get a tad irritated. It was bad enough that I had to endure the pain of these things being ripped out of my back, but to have my tormentor laughing about it was more than I could handle.

So, I asked, "What the hell is so funny back there?"

The nurse replied, "It looks like the doctor has stapled your asshole closed."

Great. That's just great. I know he gave me some bad percentages about normal bowel movements, but this is ridiculous.

Roommate Relationship

*F*lorida Atlantic University, located in Boca Raton, Florida, is considered to be an "upper division" school. That means that the curriculum is specialized. I was awarded two degrees from FAU. The first was a Bachelor's Degree in Art Education, and the second was a Master's Degree in Art, specializing in curriculum writing. That's what is meant by "upper division."

The campus of FAU is situated on an old World War Two runway. In fact, *many* of the campuses in the Florida university system are located on old, defunct World War Two runways. I suppose they got the real estate cheap — plus, most of the pavement for parking lots was already in place.

There are a number of dormitories on the FAU campus. I lived in a few of them over the years. For one quarter — they're on the "quarter" system down in Florida, as opposed to the "semester" system — I lived with all Cuban students. My roommate, in an attempt to teach me Spanish, wrote the names of everything in the room in Spanish on pieces of masking tape and stuck them everywhere. I remember the word *"puerto."* Every week they would have a wild party that they called a "tsunami." It was a great event — provided you were invited.

On one occasion, I even dated a Cuban princess. We walked off campus to have a bite to eat, and about 20 feet behind us were these two muscle-bound apes, following us. Finally, I asked the girl who the hell these mountains of flesh were following us, and she told me that they were her "chaperones," along for the night in case I did anything that they deemed improper. If I did, they would descend upon me like a red-brick building in an earthquake. That relationship didn't last long. Can you imagine what would have happened if I grabbed her breast?

So, one year, I was partnered up with a guy named Reese Wingate. Reese was a true Florida cracker. He came from the west side of the peninsula somewhere and was one of those rough-and-ready types.

They had a bar on campus called "The Rathskeller." It served only beer, but there were ways around that. Back in the '70s, Quaaludes were the drug of choice in south Florida for a while. The only problem with Quaaludes was that you tended to forget how many you'd ingested, and that could lead to a rather embarrassing situation.

One night, Reese, myself, and another chap were returning from the bar. We were walking three abreast down the vast concrete sidewalks that connected everything on campus. All of a sudden, Reese simply fell flat on his face. One moment, we were walking, and the next, Reese was out cold on the concrete. So we grabbed him under the arms and dragged him back to the dorm, where a debate ensued as to whether to call the paramedics — because old Reese was turning a sickly shade of blue.

Finally, one of the pre-med guys suggested that we prop him up in a cold shower. We did, and that seemed to revive him. When questioned, he admitted that he'd started out the evening with 12 Quaaludes. By the time he was revived in the shower, we could find only two — very soggy, I might add — Quaaludes on him.

Anyway, I lost touch with Reese after he left the university. As with everything in life, time marches on, and we go in different directions.

One night, many years later, I was sitting in a nightclub down in Fort Lauderdale — one of those places with a horseshoe-shaped bar. Suddenly, on the other side of the bar, this big ruckus broke out. Fists were flying, and people were ducking.

The entire conflagration came rolling around the bar. A guy stood up, holding another guy by the neck. He had his fist cocked back, and he was getting ready to really sock this dude when I shouted out, "Hey, Reese!"

He stopped and looked. A big smile came over his face, and he said, "Hey, Jason. Hold on, buddy. I'll be right over."

Then Reese punched this guy in the face and threw him to the floor.

He came around the bar, talking. He was wearing a white shirt, and I noticed there was a patch of blood on the front, so I pointed to it.

Reese said, "I told that fool that I didn't want any trouble. Hell, boy — I got stabbed just last week, but did he listen? Hell, no. But it's good to see you, old buddy — let's drink some 151 Rum."

Miss Saigon

*W*ater is the sworn enemy of steel ships. Especially saltwater. That explains why the U.S. Navy has to enlist the help of numerous Boatswain's Mates to maintain their ships. A Boatswain's Mate is commonly referred to as a "Deck Ape" in the Navy. They are solely responsible for the upkeep of the ship, maintaining its appearance, and keeping the water on the outside at all times.

I was stationed aboard an LST in Vietnam. We were part of the Water Transportation Fleet that moved men and materiel up into Cambodia when President Nixon was assuring the whole world that we weren't even in Cambodia.

I was what was called a "Leading Seaman." This meant that I controlled the entire stern division, consisting of 12 men. It was our job to maintain this old rust bucket called the *Luzerne County*. It had been built rather cheaply for the assault on Okinawa during World War Two, and, due to the effectiveness of the Japanese *"Kamikaze"* missions, they didn't expect these vessels to last very long, and so they had been just slapped together. Here we were, almost 30 years later, sailing this tub up the Mekong River, and fending off the elements, occasional bursts of machine-gun bullets, mortar rounds, and a few other items associated with warfare.

Maintaining a steel ship in water is a 24/7 operation. Rust never sleeps. Just think — if it did, can you imagine the nightmares rust would have? Well, if we wanted job security, we surely got it on this piece of junk. There was rust *everywhere,* including some places where it wasn't good to have rust on a seagoing vessel.

The process was fairly straightforward. We would chip the rust with a special hammer — called, appropriately enough, a "chipping hammer." Leave it to the Navy to coyly name a device for chipping rust. We also had a stiff wire brush that was used to knock off any pesky little pieces that had escaped the hammer's blows. Then we would seal the area with a paint called "Red Lead." It was red, and it contained lead — another example of the powers-that-be sitting around all day and thinking about these things. The "Red Lead" was actually orange in tonality — bright orange. After this dried, we would finish the job with standard Navy gray. I swear, there are parts of the seabed that are naval gray — entire kelp forests painted gray.

One day, we were working over the side of the ship. They had a barge that was lowered by crane, and we used ropes to tow it around the ship. A "Jacob's Ladder" was rolled out over the side, and that was how you would access the barge.

We spent a good part of three days while moored in Saigon painting out the rust spots on the side of this rust bucket. On the final day, we were readying to pull out and make a run up the Mekong River into Cambodia — or, maybe I should say, "Never-Neverland," so the censors aren't inclined to cringe.

I asked for a paint roller and a bucket of "Red Lead." Then I proceeded to paint a giant nude woman down the side of the ship, all 365 feet of it, on the starboard side. It was a reclining nude and was well endowed with the attributes that make a woman titillating. I placed her hand behind her head, in a "Come Hither"-type look. It worked out really well. The U.S. Navy should hire more artistic types for their warships. We could impart a little zing to a rather dull gray vessel from time to time.

At any rate, we pulled up the barge and set sail for parts unknown in Southeast Asia. The problem that became apparent were the Vietnamese in their little *sampans,* rowing by and pointing.

Some of the officers were taking this as a sort of compliment, thinking that they had finally won over the hearts and minds of the local population without having to use extremely sensitive .50 caliber machine guns. They were paying homage to us by waving their arms and pointing, but only a select few knew the truth, and they were bound to secrecy under punishment by death if they told anyone about our girlfriend.

She was a beauty, but, more importantly, no one knew what was going on. How could you see the side of the ship when you were on the top of it? Unless you sailed past a long, drawn-out mirror, there was no way of knowing that this "Red Lead Redhead" was gracing the side of this nasty-looking man o' war.

Everything was going just fine. My one-man show was becoming quite popular with the natives, and offers were streaming in from Hanoi to do a one-man show up there, with bomb craters arranged artistically. Then we stopped in Cambodia.

This proved to be my downfall. The Big Cheese and his subordinate, The Little Cheese, decided to visit one of their favorite whorehouses and had the dinghy dropped over the side. They roared out onto the river, made an abrupt U-turn, and roared right back. It was bad enough that they had to give up the golden opportunity to receive a sexually transmitted disease — now, they had to come back aboard to arrange the keel-hauling or plank-walking ceremonies for the next day.

Once they finished with the 50 lashes, which rendered my lower back the texture of ground beef, they told me in no uncertain terms that I — and I alone — would be responsible for painting that entire ship gray. They were asking me to cover up my mural — *such barbarians!*

I thought about leaving just one breast exposed as a reminder of this brilliant piece of work, but I decided at the last minute that they didn't deserve a talent of my magnitude. I think that Nero and Hitler must have felt the same way!

Hey, Sailor Man!

*P*art of my stint with the U.S. Navy was spent at the Philadelphia Shipyard. I was stationed there for a few months prior to being sent over to Vietnam.

The one good thing about being stationed in Philadelphia was the fact that it was a two-hour bus ride from there to Wilkes-Barre, the town I grew up in. In *Urban Gothic,* the first book in this series, I had a story called "Tony's Cadillac," about how a bunch of us would chip in and drive up there in this huge black Caddie, owned by a guy named Tony. But the episode I'm about to relate happened before that, when I was still riding Martz Trailways, aka "The Bus."

Usually, I would leave on a Friday afternoon, arriving in good ol' W-B by about 7:00 pm, and then return with the latest bus I could get on Sunday. That would put me at the Philadelphia bus station around 9:00 pm. Now that I think about it, this probably wasn't the smartest thing to do. Philadelphia had a notorious reputation back then — especially in the 1970s — for violent crime. It was something that then-mayor Rizzo had promised to clean up, and he actually did.

I occasionally ran into Rizzo's men on the street. They never messed with me because I was always in uniform, but they were a force to be reckoned with. Rizzo dressed them up in black leather jackets, with black leather jackboots. They would "dress" their pants, meaning that they would tuck them into their boots. These guys looked like Gestapo, which was the idea, I suppose. They would knuckle your head and *then* ask you your name, but the city needed this, because the violence situation was serious.

So, there I am, getting off the bus at 9:00 pm in downtown Philadelphia. For some reason, there was a walk to get to the other, local, bus stop that would take me out to the Naval Base on South Broad Street.

I was walking through the bus station with my seabag over my shoulder. Yes, that's right — my seabag. We carried everything we owned in that one canvas bag. It weighed 66 pounds when it was fully packed. In boot camp, they had a special class to teach us how to pack that bag. It was really incredible how much actually fit into the thing.

I had a couple pair of shoes, underwear, T-shirts, two complete uniforms, a shaving kit and a sewing kit, all government-issue. That evening, I was dressed in my dress blues, which meant that I was wearing my peacoat. It was a big black woolen thing that left your neck exposed to the elements. There was a top button, but it would scratch your neck if you used it.

So, there I was — a nice, uniformed sailor boy hiking through this bus station at night in downtown Philadelphia.

Suddenly, a guy stepped out of the shadows. He was short and wearing a mismatched wardrobe, like something put together at The Salvation Army Store. He had those eyes that looked in two directions. You never know which eyeball to focus on when confronted with one of these people. I think it's caused by an optical-muscle problem — that's the reason the guy's eyes wandered a bit.

The guys comes up alongside me and starts to keep pace with me. Then he said to me, "Hey, sailorman. You wanna buy something dat will keep youse warm all night?"

At first, I thought about telling him to piss off, but he really wasn't threatening me, so I just kept walking. He persisted, though. He kept pace with me and kept asking, "Hey, sailorman. You wanna buy something dat will keep youse warm all night?"

This went on for about 50 yards or so, him walking alongside me and asking the same question: "Hey, sailorman. You wanna buy somethin' that'll keep youse warm all night?"

Naturally, I thought he was talking about his sister or possibly one of his girls. Hell, I didn't know. But it was starting to really annoy me as time went on.

Then we came up on this concrete buttress, and behind it was a beat-up cardboard box. He went over there and started to rummage around and then came back with this package. Again, he said, "Sailorman — wanna buy somethin' that'll keep you warm all night?"

He was holding a really cheap electric blanket.

Gourmet Snow

*F*or three years, I worked as an advertising salesman for an art magazine in West Palm Beach, Florida. It was the sister publication of *Arts Magazine*, out of New York, and was called *Art Voices South*.

I sold both color and black-and-white advertising to art galleries and related businesses all around the United States, using what were called "Watts Lines." They were the precursor to 800 numbers that have become a staple of American business everywhere.

I must tell you this: I was really good at what I did and sold a lot of advertising. Part of my weekly salary depended on it as a commission and a draw — a commission that paid 3% of the price of the ad, which could be substantial, because full-page color advertising was not cheap in this magazine.

All of this newfound wealth found its way into my personal coffers and allowed me to live the

South Florida lifestyle — sports car, pineapple shirts, and sandals.

During this period, I became interested in gourmet cooking. One of my specialties, to which I'd come back time and time again, was duck in an orange sauce — flambéed duck in orange sauce.

I would spend the entire week looking for the choice ingredients for my Saturday ritual — the finest fresh duck and Florida oranges. I even invested in a bottle of *Kirschwasser*, a German liqueur that was in the rocket-fuel family. This was used to flambé the poor duck with that captivating blue flame, imparting a crispness to the skin that only a good flambé can accomplish.

After a leisurely start, I would begin the Saturday ritual by preparing the duck. Then, I would render the fresh orange sauce using vast amounts of sugar and orange juice. During this entire process, the vodka and tonic would be flowing. Toward the afternoon, my friend Denis would stop by, and he and I would invest in cocaine. Every week, we had the same good intention — we would start with a few good cocktails and then supplement that with a number of nice lines of choice Florida toot. After the first gram was exhausted, one of us would dash out to Louie's and buy some more. They always said that you should snort cocaine will a C-note so that you have enough money for the next gram, so this is precisely what we did. We used a number of $100 bills.

During that period, I was married to a Roman Catholic. She was a good person, but I had this thing about Catholicism because I'd spent 12 years in a catholic school. Trust me, the Sisters of Mercy were far from "merciful" back then. They beat the living crap out of me. Sure, it's easy for you to say that I probably deserved these weekly beatings, but that wasn't quite true. Once they beat my left hand because I used it to write with, and they felt that it was Satan's own handwriting that issued forth from a "southpaw."

So, I married a Roman Catholic. It would amaze me that here she was, a true clothes horse who worked for some hotshot attorney. But, once a year, she would walk around all day with dirt on her forehead. Plus the palm fronds hanging around the house — that was always rich.

This woman drank scotch. I would buy her Ballantine's 12 Year Old, and that bottle would sit there on the counter for months. I never understood that. I would tell her that it was going to go bad if she didn't drink it. It didn't matter. A little scotch on the rocks after work, and the cork would go back into the jug. Whereas I — hell, the first thing I did when I opened a bottle of liquor was to throw away the lid — what was the sense? It wasn't going to last long enough, anyway, so why be bothered with placing the cap back on after use?

Here she was — Miss Goody Two Shoes, churchgoer, Holy Molly with a smudge on her forehead.

But, when it came to cocaine — forget it. She was like a *Hoover*. The entire line would go up into her nose in a jiff. Even the tablecloth wasn't safe — if she fell off the mirror, it would get sucked into the straw. I never did quite figure that one out. Denis and I would just sit back and say, "Wow! That is one nasty honker you have there, lady!"

There we were, snorting lines and drinking booze, and, all the while, I was gourmet-cooking a duck. The orange sauce would go over the animal, and into the oven it went. Every few minutes, I would pull it out to spread the juices over the surface in order to achieve a nice tan. I even went out and bought one of those squeeze balls for this purpose.

Finally, at the very end, I would pour on the

Kirschwasser and light that mother up. It was beautiful, the blue flames licking the range hood and casting an eerie glow throughout the kitchen. We would turn off all the lights for this grand finale.

Here is where the ridiculous part comes in. If you've ever partaken of copious amounts of cocaine, you know that appetite virtually vanishes. None of us were in the least bit interested in eating this fine meal. We would sit there, chopping out another line, admiring the perfect skin of the basted duck, poking at the leg or pushing the wild rice around on the plate but not touching a morsel of food.

Finally, the coke would run out, and we would bid our adieus for the evening, swearing that next Saturday would be different — we would actually eat dinner next week *for sure!*

I would go in and wrap everything in tin foil. It would then get pushed to the back of the refrigerator until Thursday night, when it was garbage day. Friday, I would start the same thing all over again.

In some of the circles that I now run in, they say that insanity is doing the same thing over and over again while expecting a different outcome. If that it a viable definition, then it would be correct to assume that we were acting

under the definition of a completely insane
flambéed duck.

With a Song in My Head

*O*ne night when I had just turned 14 years old, I was plowing snow with my father. He was driving his brand-new Ford pickup truck with a snowplow attachment. The truck was "fire-engine red."

As we sped down this country road pushing snow over to the side, I said to him, "When I get old enough, I'm going to leave and never come back. I'm going to live somewhere that doesn't even know that snow exists."

He wasn't the least bit happy with my proclamation, because he had big plans for me to continue working for him as an indentured servant. I hated snow. Oh, sure, snow is nice when you have plenty of dough and you can go play in it, but to have to work in that stuff is another story entirely. It gets dirty really fast, and then it doesn't look as pretty — and it's colder than hell.

Actually, according to Dante, that is incorrect.

In his *Inferno*, he mentions the 14 levels of
hell, the last being cold and ice, because it was
the furthest away from God's eternal love and
warmth. Although I have heard that the devil
is a cheap bastard and keeps his thermostat
turned way down so he doesn't have to spend
extra money on heating oil. And that is also
true — hell is heated with oil. Just think about
it: all of the greed and death surrounding
the oil industry, plus what we're doing to the
environment by using oil — that all spells
involvement by good ol' Lucifer himself.

   Back to the story.

   At the age of 19, I enlisted in the U.S. Navy
and got sent to Vietnam — in January. It was
hot as — well, you know: hell. It was then that
I realized that places existed that had never
heard of snow.

   In 1972, I moved with my first wife to south
Florida — Boca Raton, to be exact. I enrolled
at Florida Atlantic University and kept going
back for the next 10 years, earning a number
of college degrees in the process. Being that
I'd pissed off my old man by leaving his
employment embrace, he wasn't about to pay
a dime toward my college education. He then
got into cahoots with my Uncle Sam, who also
decided not to help out with my education.

So I ended up putting my skills as a heavy-equipment operator to work to earn money for college.

I worked for a number of firms over the years in south Florida. Most of the time, I was engaged in the act of ruining the place by building pads for new houses. When I first got to south Florida, the Everglades were pretty far west of town. Went I left, the city went right up and into those same Everglades. It was like taking a rolling pin and flattening a big city, pushing it out in all directions until you have a really big city that occupies a huge amount of land. Sorry to say, I was instrumental in doing this just so I could get an education.

Because of the location, we were always working in the boondocks of Florida, way out there where the trains don't run and the buses turn around. We would dig these giant lakes to create dirt to raise the houses four feet above the flood plain. They would then sell the lots as waterfront. But beware of swimming in them. The side walls go straight down to a depth of at least 1000 feet or more. These don't have any beaches attached to them.

There were two ways to dig these lakes. The first was to use what is called a "drag line." This instrument of destruction consists of a steam shovel with a big bucket on the end of a cable. You throw it out there and then drag it in, loaded with dirt. Hence, the term "drag line."

The second way to dig a lake is the way we did them. You get a bunch of machines called "Earthmovers." These have a belly pan that drops down and scoops up copious quantities of dirt and hauls it to the top. They do this all day, in and out of a hole in the ground, scooping dirt and dropping it off. My job consisted of either one of these two. I either pushed these monsters around so that they could really get a belly full of dirt or flattened that dirt on the other end by smoothing it out for your grandmother's little retirement house to be built on.

Here's where it gets complicated.

I remember reading a study once that claimed that the human brain works at a certain RPM level. When this is coupled with a certain low-decibel noise, like the engine of a D-8 Caterpillar bulldozer, you get very creative thoughts. I am not making this up. The noise, wedded to a certain number of revolutions per minute, produces the ingredients for deep, serious thought waves. Or I should say, "brain waves and subsequent thought processes." Go ahead — look it up. Hell, all you need is a phone to do that nowadays.

Well, a D-8 Caterpillar bulldozer runs at about 800 RPMs, and the engine emits a low growl. I used to sit there all day long and listen to this. This was fine for creative thought, but when a certain song would impose itself on those aforementioned brain waves, well, then you have a problem.

One day, Bobby Darin's "Splish Splash (I Was Takin' a Bath)" got stuck inside my head. It played over and over again. *"Splish, splash, I was takin' a bath/all about a Saturday night/Rub-a-dub, I was relaxin' in the tub/thinking everything was alright…"* You get the picture, or should I say, you hear the sound track. There I was, in the middle of nowhere, sitting on a bulldozer the size of a common retirement home in south Florida, with this ridiculous song stuck in my head.

Finally, I stopped the Pan operator and begged him to lend me his headphones so I could replace the song in my head before I went completely mad. He understood me perfectly. He knew what I was talking about when I told him about this phenomenon.

There are ways to prevent this from happening, one of which is what I'm doing right now. I'm using that hard-won college

education to type these words on a page —
rather than sit on a huge bulldozer and push
dirt around all day with some unwanted song
playing in my head.

Buried Alive

*B*ack when I was growing up, my father had a coal business. We delivered coal to people's houses so that they could heat and cook their meals with the stuff. Everyone had a coal-fired furnace or a kitchen coal stove back then. Of course, living in Wilkes-Barre had something to do with it, seeing as how, at one time, it was the capital of the anthracite coal industry.

We had two trucks that were called "high lift" trucks. This meant that they had a big box on the back that lifted several tons of coal into the air so that we could take advantage of gravity and slide the coal into people's basements. Through a series of hydraulic pistons and giant metal scissors, the truck would tilt the "body" and then lift it straight into the air. Then we hooked up these aluminum chutes on the back and directed the coal into a little window under the porch.

Usually, people would want to fill up their coal bins during the summer, when there wasn't a high demand for coal because of the temperature. What would happen is that we'd end up delivering 10 or 12 tons to the same address, filling their coal bin to the rafters. This meant that one person had to be outside with the controls, and the other poor bastard was in the coal bin, shoveling his head off, keeping the coal away from the end of the chute so that we could get as much in as possible.

Normally, one of my brothers would be the poor bastard, but during this time, we were actually phasing out the coal business and going into just the trucking business. So, I was shorthanded.

I had a friend named Louis. He was a really nice guy. The only problem with Louis was the fact that he loved his hashish. He didn't go anywhere without his hash pipe.

So, being hard up for an employee, I asked Louis to act as a paid helper on my coal truck, and he agreed.

We started out at this house in Wilkes-Barre. I knew the house, and I knew the coal bin. I had shoveled many a ton of coal into this particular basement. I backed the truck up and hooked up the chutes. Then I lifted the four tons of coal into the air. I took Louis down into the basement and pointed out what his position was.

I said, "Louis, do you see that little window up there with a chute sticking out of it? Well, in a few minutes, tons of black, dirty, and really wet coal are going to start issuing forth from that window. Your job is to shovel like mad and keep that coal from filling up the area directly under the chute. Do you have it?"

Louis assured me that he understood completely the task at hand. He would stand there and shovel his head off until all of the coal was in the bin.

Then I went topside and started running the coal in. Every now and then, I would stop and yell down to Louis, "Hey, Louis, are youse OK down there?"

He would answer, "Yeah, I'm doin' good. Keep it comin'."

Then I'd run in some more coal, stop, and ask the same question. Louis would respond accordingly, and we would continue.

After a while, I started to get suspicious. I knew this coal bin, and I knew how furiously you had to shovel to keep up with the chute. Plus, I started to hear this hysterical laughter issuing from the basement window.

After a while, I couldn't take it any longer. I knew something was wrong, so I stopped the flow of coal and hiked around the back of the house, into the basement.

The sight I was met with was terrible. There was my friend Louis, buried up to his armpits in black, dirty, and extremely wet coal. The area of the coal bin where the coal should have been was completely empty. I had to break down the wooden barrier that held the coal in and free Louis from the cold, black, wet embrace. While I was doing this, he continued to laugh like a madman.

Finally, after a lot of extra work, cleaning up the basement floor, and even mopping up the black coal water, I asked Louis what the hell had happened.

He explained to me that he was "getting off" on being buried in coal.

The moral of this story is relatively simple: Don't hire a friend named Louis, who has a hash pipe that never goes cold, and expect him to be rational about coal deliveries.

Of course, when you think of it, there's nothing rational about coal deliveries to begin with.

No Preference

*A*s mentioned in other stories, I was stationed at the U.S. Navy Shipyard in Philadelphia, Pennsylvania, back in 1969.

There I was, just minding my own business, walking around base with a Vicks inhaler crammed full of Amylnitrate (RE) — aka, "poppers" — bouncing off the chain-link fence that surrounded the compound.

One day, I received orders to report for duty in the country of South Vietnam. Suddenly, my days of *"Two dead men on a dead man's chest"* came screaming to a halt. I had been given what was assumed to be at that time a sure-fire death certificate: Go to a country where there was a very real, very active war taking place; for some reason, they needed me there. I thought long and hard on the subject, and I couldn't come up with any viable reason that I should go to Vietnam, but the Navy thought otherwise.

Prior to shipping out, I was ordered to go

running around the base having a number of issues resolved. They sent me to the medical people to have a physical. It wouldn't have been in their best interests to send me there with a cold or some exotic sexually transmitted disease — I wouldn't be in position to get killed correctly. I also had to get several injections, one of which was an anti-lead enzyme that was supposed to keep bullets away from me. The other 28 shots would protect me from those nasty Asian bugs like malaria, beriberi, and head lice.

I did all of this — ran around the base *sans* my canister of Vicks inhalant, taking care of all the things on my extensive list, until, one day, I came up against a real puzzler — the identification room.

I stood there for about an hour. The line was moving very slowly, and, soon, I found out why. Finally, it was my turn to step up to the little window. Seated behind the sliding trap door was this very rotund individual. She was wearing a pair of those eyeglasses that were big in the 1950s. You know the kind — they had these wings that flipped out on both sides and were a bright-purple color. She was chewing gum, too — not some wimpy breath product but real Double Bubble stuff, the kind you used to blow bubbles the size of watermelons with.

Finally, she inserted these two small metal blanks into her machine. This thing was huge. It had all of these belts and levers, black metal with chrome keys, and it made a humming noise. Once she got it all set up, the questions started.

"Name."

"J-A-S-O-N G-O-O-D-M-A-N."

The keys flew out and *Thud! Ticka! Thud! Ticka! Thud!* She was actually typing on metal!

"Rank."

"Blood Type."

"Navy serial number."

"What religion are you?"

I thought for a moment and said, "Well, I'm a pantheist."

She cracked her chewing gum and said, "What?"

"I said that I'm a pantheist."

She said, "Listen, smart guy. Youse can either be Kat-lick, Jewish, or Protestant — and yeah, you can say, 'No Preference.' Make up your mind, pal. We's got ah lot of people in line. Today would be appreciated."

I gave her my answer. The machine went *Thud! Ticka! Thud! Ticka! Thud!*

To this day, my dog tags say, "No Preference."

Montego Bay Episode

*D*uring the '70s, I was in and out of Boca Raton, Florida, while working on my university degrees. Back then, air travel was still relatively cheap, so I took advantage of this by flying back and forth from Manhattan to West Palm Beach on an almost-regular basis. Another convenient destination was the Caribbean.

After every scholastic accomplishment, I would congratulate myself with a trip to the islands. I started to fly down to Jamaica.

Montego Bay was a nice little town back then. It wasn't built up with singles' resorts yet, and the place had a sleepy, laid-back feeling to it. Another plus was the rum. I could buy a quart of really nice Honduran or Cuban rum for a song. The Coca Cola that went into a tall, cold drink was much more expensive than the rum. At $1.25 per quart of rum, it was easy to stay half buzzed all day long in Montego Bay.

I usually stayed at Mrs. G's Hotel. It was a

small place stuck on the side of a hill just outside of town. It had everything that a young, up-and-coming guy could ask for: An outdoor dining room, a nice, kidney-shaped pool, and a waiter in a little red jacket with a black bow tie who brought a silver ice bucket and two Coca Colas to my room whenever I asked.

On one of my trips — I went there four times over the years — I was in town just walking around when a Rasty Man approached me and asked me if I wanted to buy a carved coconut shell. He looked at my bloodshot eyes and said, "No, mon. You not want any tourist-junk souvenirs. He said that if I were to give him $15 — Yankee dollars — he could buy a pound of pot and supplies to take me up into the Blue Mountains to stay at his house for a few weeks. So, being young and stupid, I agreed.

The next morning, I checked out of Mrs. G's Hotel and proceeded to go to our pre-arranged meeting place.

Then I waited.

And waited.

Until I came to the conclusion that my $15 — Yankee dollars — had gone to the Blue Mountains alone. Just as I was walking away, there was a tug on my shirtsleeve, and there was "Mashu," smiling. He apologized to me because the pound of pot, that pound of really good Jamaican dope, had cost him $12 instead of the $10 he'd quoted me. That's where he'd been — negotiating on my behalf with his supplier.

We started our journey into the Blue Mountains. He showed me what bus to get on. There I was, stuffed into this bus with people holding goats, piglets, and children, all of them squealing and shouting at the same time. It was hot and dusty, and we went flying up this narrow two-lane road. On two or three occasions, you could hear the horn blaring just in time to see a huge truck careening around a blind curve. I swear, I almost soiled my trousers, especially when I looked and saw an 800-foot drop-off on our right side. It dawned on me that the drop-off should have been on the left because they drive on the left in Jamaica. But no one seemed upset except me. They were talking and laughing, pretty much ignoring the dumb gringo in their midst.

We got to Mashu's house, way up into the mountains. It was really a complex of three buildings; one of them was his and another my sleeping room. There was a smaller outbuilding that he used for his cooking and *spliff*-making place. The buildings were interesting. Each was

a simple framed structure built up on stilts.
Inside, the studs were exposed, and they had
only these shutters for windows. There wasn't
any glass. The most striking thing I remember
was the floors. Each place had a floor that was
stained and heavily varnished like a good piece
of furniture. There must have been 10 coats
of varnish on these floors. They *shined.* Every
morning, Mashu would wipe the floor down
with a soft cloth. It was almost a ritual.

The other activity was the *spliff*-rolling. He
would take about a quarter-ounce of pot and
roll it into a huge *spliff.* This, he smoked while
preparing his "cow horn" water pipe. You have
to keep in mind that the Rastafarians consider
ganja to be a spiritual experience.

And after a stay with this guy in the Blue
Mountains, I concurred.

Mashu would fire up this pipe and
hyperventilate until there was a huge blue
cloud of smoke around his head. Then he'd
inhale for what seemed like 10 minutes, pulling
all of that smoke into his lungs. Then he'd sit
there, holding it in. This went on every single
day — sometimes a few times a day. To him, it
was like going to church.

A few nights, we trekked through the jungle
over to a small "bar." It was a shack that served

warm Guinness Stout in pony bottles, had a huge Wurlitzer jukebox — with only two records in it. Four sides of nice reggae music. After a few hours of Guinness and a *spliff*, it didn't matter much that they kept on playing the same four songs.

His friend, "Spider," was hanging upside-down from a tree that sat next to the building, and we all just flowed with the rhythm until it was time to climb back over hill and dale for a night's rest.

After two weeks, it was time to leave. Mashu was stuffing pot into an old cornmeal box. I had a difficult time trying to explain to him why I couldn't possibly pass through Miami International Airport with that in my bag. He truly did not understand why.

Come to think of it, it still doesn't make any sense.

Dining Out in Saigon

*A*fter a 22-hour flight, we arrived in Saigon — at Tung Son Ut Airport, to be exact. The first thing that hit us was the heat and humidity. It was like running into a damp, hot wall.

Naturally, we stood around for hours in a hangar, waiting for the powers-that-be to decide where they were going to take us. Finally, a couple of military buses arrived, and we all climbed onboard. I knew something was wrong when I looked out the window and saw a soldier in full combat attire walking around with a mirror on the end of a stick, looking very carefully at the underside of the bus.

They drove us downtown, to the Hotel Annapolis. This was the U.S. Navy's in-country indoctrination center. We were to stay here for the next two weeks being educated in the ways of war.

About two weeks prior to our arrival, a bomb

had blown part of the building clean off. That particular part had housed the mess hall and a few administrative offices. They said that a number of personnel had lost their lives in that explosion, which was attributed to the Viet Cong.

What that meant was this: we had to walk down the street, approximately a quarter of a mile, to the U.S. Army chow hall. So, at every mealtime, three times a day, there we were, double-file, walking down this foul-smelling street, exposed to anyone who might be driving by on a moped, past concrete emplacements with machine-gun barrels sticking out of the little windows.

One morning while walking to breakfast, an old woman came up and stood on the curb with her ass pointed toward the street. She proceeded to hike up her dress, squat down, and take a crap — right there in front of us. Then she just stood up and walked away. There was this steaming pile of choice Vietnamese shit lying in the gutter. A few of our number decided that they had to watch their caloric intake that morning and were not interested in breakfast.

In the Navy, they treat their men quite well when it comes to food. That old song that goes

"The Navy gets the gravy/and the Army gets the beans" is fairly accurate. I was accustomed to asking for my eggs to be done in a particular way, such as, "I'll have two over easy this morning." And that's what I did. I walked into this Army mess hall and looked at the green eggs. They always looked green because they were powdered eggs, probably left over from World War Two. So I decided I would ask for two eggs over easy that morning.

It was a big mistake.

Hidden behind a tarp that acted as a wall of sorts was the Army Master Sergeant who operated this mess hall. He was classic, even down to the tattoo that said "Mom" on his arm. He stepped out and looked at me. A look of disgust passed over his face when he saw my blue "Sand Pebbles" uniform. The young cookie had this frightened look on his face. It was as if Godzilla was standing behind me and I didn't know about it — the cook's face was pure fear. The Master Sergeant placed his hands on his hips and said, "Did I hear you correctly? You asked for two eggs over easy?"

I responded by saying, "You are absolutely correct, sir. Those scrambled eggs look a bit peaked this morning, so I thought I'd try something different."

That was the wrong answer.

The Master Sergeant walked over and relieved the young guy in front of the greasy bacon and green eggs. He said, "Listen — it's bad enough that you faggot, pussy-faced sailor boys come into *my* chow hall. *That,* I can't do anything about. But when youse come in here, requesting special-order items from my men, then that is where we draw the line. It's your lucky day, squib. I'm gonna give you the privilege of my serving you breakfast this morning, so, let's get started — shall we?"

Then he grabbed a stainless-steel tray and started shoveling the green scrambled eggs on it in a heap.

"We will start this little culinary episode with some of our award-winning scrambled eggs. As a special treat, I'm gonna add one of our special ingredients, a little yellow mustard. On top of that, keeping your nutritional requirements in the forefront, we'll add a little chocolate sauce to bring out the complex flavors of this exquisite dish. And now, I will include a nice, heaping portion of our finest smoked bacon, which has been fried in extra grease, to give you the complete dining experience. And to top it all off — if that's even possible — I'm going to have a seat with you and watch you eat every delicious morsel of this carefully prepared food."

He was serious — dead serious. He walked around the steam trays with a mug of coffee, and he had his guy place this tray in front of me.

It was like eating out of a dumpster.

I sat down, and this big, ugly Master Sergeant sat across from me, puffing on his cheap cigar and saying, "Go ahead. Enjoy the fruits of my tireless labor. We always really appreciate having youse Navy boys come in here and critique our little café from time to time. It keeps us on our toes, you might say."

I started to eat the stuff around the edges, trying to avoid the chocolate sauce dripping down from the top of the green pile.

Fortunately, the Master Sergeant was called away. It seemed there was a problem with the botulism-injection system out back. It proved to be my opportunity to escape with my stomach intact.

Every meal after that, I had to sneak up to the entrance and make sure my antagonist wasn't anywhere to be seen before going in for breakfast.

My suggestion is this: If you have a choice between the Navy and the Army for a dinner date, by all means — choose the Navy.

Another Day at Rocco's Bar

I don't know what all the fuss is about these sports bars.

In my hometown, a sports bar was simply a gin mill where the patrons were into sports — usually all of the sports. Now, granted, you would be pretty hard pressed to put hunting up on a jumbo screen — or fishing, for that matter. Talk about a really boring afternoon. Watching videos of guys walking through woods or standing in a creek, getting their lines wet.

But at Rocco's bar, they were into *all* of the sports. You name it, they did it. Baseball, football, basketball, fishing, hunting — hell, they used to fly down to the Carolinas just to play golf. On one occasion, they all got together and went up to Muhammad Ali's camp in the Poconos just to say "Hello." That's true — Ali had a house and his workout center not far from Larksville, Pennsylvania. He used to chop wood to build up his shoulders. All the wood he used to heat his home with, he cut by hand. They told me that he was a really nice guy.

But, getting back to Rocco's Bar.

During hunting season, that was where the really weird stuff would happen.

The Rocco brothers were great jokesters. In fact, they would go to great lengths to pull off the perfect joke. One day, Tony and the boys came in from hunting small game. They had all bagged a couple of rabbits and were really full of themselves. Tony excused himself and went into the back. When he came out he set one of his dead rabbits up on a barstool and then produced his shotgun.

He yelled out, "There's the sonofabitch! I'll get him!" With that, he cut loose with both barrels. The rabbit flew across the room, and everyone was scrambling for cover.

What Tony had done was remove all the pellets from two shotgun shells. But he left the wads in, so that, when he shot the gun, the wads blew the rabbit off the stool. After we had all recuperated, we had a bunch of laughs at Tony's indoor small-game hunt.

On another occasion, they all came back from the woods. Let me just add that the woods were about a mile away. It didn't take much to get into the woods around these parts. You just stuck your license on your back, grabbed your gun, and hiked up the mountain to go hunting.

This time, they came back with grouse and a couple of ring necks. These were the game birds that roamed the forests of northeastern Pennsylvania. Some guy was there who started to argue with Tony about one of his birds. He said something that we weren't quite privy to, but Tony jumped up, grabbed a grouse, and said, "You're on, buddy. Just get your money on the bar."

With that, Tony disappeared into the back room. We heard a *Chop!* and soon he reappeared with the head of the bird. He brought it in and shoved it into his glass of beer and proceeded to use it as a straw. He was sucking his beer up through the throat of this dead bird. It was completely insane. There was the beak at the bottom and these beady little eyes staring out. Then Tony made the sound like the bottom of a milkshake cup — that unmistakable sucking sound. I think his brother Bob had to go and hurl after that one.

Tony never did tell us the full transcript of the argument, but, whatever it was, he was $10 richer afterwards.

Flying Circus

*F*lorida isn't a bad place to live for a while.

I spent more than 18 years in south Florida between the towns of Boca Raton and Palm Beach. Two of my college degrees came from Florida Atlantic University in Boca Raton, and I lived there off and on while attending classes. For a few years, I lived in a little part of Boynton Beach that juts out into the ocean. I had a house about 200 yards from the beach and could hear the surf crashing at night when I was lying in bed. It was a neat, little, secret beach community with some really weird people in it.

My Dad used to pop down in the wintertime, alone, and would suggest, "Let's go to an island somewhere." So I would book us flights to whatever island struck our fancy at the time. On one occasion, we chose the islands of Turks and Caicos, down below Cuba. We booked a

cheap flight with an airline called Air Florida. It
no longer exists. They were the guys who had
oxygen canisters aboard without telling anyone.
It turned out that these things were highly
flammable, similar to the type that the ill-fated
Russian sailors used on the nuclear-powered
submarine *Kursk*. As soon as these things strike
water, they explode in a ball of fire.

Now this begs the question: Why would you
put emergency oxygen equipment that explodes
when it hits water *on a submarine?* Hmmm.
Interesting question — and one that will go
unanswered, since all aboard died.

And that is exactly what happened on that
Air Florida flight. The 0_2 canisters exploded in
the cargo hold of a jet, and it went down in the
Everglades with everyone on board — a terrible
air tragedy.

Well, this was the same airline that my Dad
and I were booked on. Fortunately, that Air
Florida accident had not yet taken place.

The Big Duke and I touched down on Caicos
Island and booked a room or two for a week. It
was the perfect place to go if you want to get
away from everything and everyone. Back in
the early 1980s, there was absolutely nothing
there.

There were only two hotels. The larger one

had a nice restaurant and bar. They would post the dinner specials out front after 4:00 pm, because that's when the flight would come in and determine what they were going to serve that evening.

You could almost hear some little guy wearing a ridiculous outfit yelling out, *"Dee plan! Dee plan!"*

What happened was that the plane would bring in the fresh provisions to the island. So, if they landed with steak on board, then they served steak. If it was pork chops, then they served that. What I could never understand was that the waters around these islands were teeming with lobster — well, spiny lobster, anyway. But the natives won't go near that water. I never did get an answer to that question.

We putzed around, hitting the beach, cruising around on the few miles of dirt roads they had, and just generally doing what you do on a tropical island — not much.

In the evening, I would get dressed and walk over to the bar at the other hotel. One night, I was in there, getting really tuned up — the liquor was flowing. The owners placed everyone's bottle of booze on the bar and told everyone to serve themselves because

he wanted to come around and join us; there
was a real "impromptu party" feeling to the
whole night. I was drinking hard with this one
guy, and we ended up staggering back to the
other hotel about 3:00 am, singing every song
we could conjure up and even making a few
up. The next morning, we were flying back
to Miami, so I wanted to get my licks in that
evening, and I was not disappointed.

The next morning, we showed up at the
airport and boarded our plane in preparation
for takeoff. We were sitting way up front in
two of the bulkhead seats when the door to the
cockpit opened and out stepped the co-pilot.
Yep — you guessed it: the same guy who'd
staggered back with me the night before.

Naturally, I didn't tell my old man about this.
He'd always hated drinking — with a passion.
He was a true "Never did, never will" type of
guy.

We exchanged salutations and smiled at each
other. The Duke asked me where I knew him
from, and I said that this was a small island,
wasn't it?

The runway on the island of Caicos is very
small, but more disconcerting is the fact that
it is short. When we took off, the guy just
yanked back on the stick, and we went up in a

45-degree ascent. He had that thing wide open; you could hear those engines just screaming back there.

What happened was the drink cart broke loose from its securing straps and went careening down the center aisle, just missing my Dad's shoulder. That would have pissed him off — getting busted up by a drink cart full of miniatures. They got it secured, and we flew on.

When we got near Miami, they placed us in a holding pattern. We flew around and around in measured circles for about 15 minutes. Then the captain came on and said that we had to fly to the Bahamas because we were running out of gas. So we flew over to Nassau and landed near the self-serve pump. Then the co-pilot, my drinking buddy from the night before, came out with his hat in hand, looking for cash. I am not making this up.

I asked him what the problem was. He briefly explained that they had only so much fuel onboard and it didn't allow for too many minutes of joyriding over Miami. So, basically, we ran out of gas. But the problem at hand was the fact that the guys in the gas station wouldn't take their credit card. So they were looking for cash money in exchange for some cheap flight vouchers as well as hitting up the stewardesses for the dough from the errant drink cart.

   Finally it was resolved, but let me tell you: I never had much faith in Air Florida again. When a gas station rejects your credit card for jet fuel, you need either a new business plan or more investors.

Sleepus Interruptus

*E*verything is old in Philadelphia.
It is one of the oldest cities in the United
States, just behind Saint Augustine, Florida.
The Navy Shipyard in Philadelphia is old, just
like the rest of the city. I was stationed there
prior to being shipped out to Vietnam. We were
housed in the old red-brick barracks — those
things dated back to the Revolutionary War. In
fact, I wouldn't be surprised if I found out that
the British troops were bivouacked there before
they were sent packing.

The red-brick barracks were three stories and
did not have elevators. Inside, wood floors were
all something that yuppies would die for if they
saw them. Actually, they were a pain in the
ass, because, being a Boatswain's Mate, I was
assigned to keeping them clean and shiny.

A few hundred yards down the way stood our
cafeteria. Three times a day, we would walk
down there to have our meals. But the thing

about walking around a Navy base is this: if you passed an officer, someone with "scrambled eggs" on their hat (please refer to the story *Cold Beer Duct* for an explanation of the term "scrambled eggs" as referring to rank in the U.S. Navy), you were supposed to say, "By your way, sir." If they walked by and you didn't say those magic words, they would make you do 50 pushups right there on the spot, in any kind of weather.

Once you got to the mess hall, assuming that you didn't have mud all over your chest from doing pushups in the rain, when the cookies saw your rank on your sleeve, they would mess with you. That's why they call it a "mess hall." At the time, I was a lowly Seaman. But some of the guys were mere Seaman Apprentices, which was even worse. Let's just say that these cooks were a pain.

One day, the guy had a nice piece of blueberry pie on his spatula. My tray was full of food — meat and potatoes, gravy, and peas. He asked me if I wanted a nice piece of pie. I said, "Yes, *Sir!*" He then proceeded to flip the pie upside down into my gravy and mashed spuds. Then I had to say, "Thank you, *Sir!*"

Bastards.

The old brick barracks were loud. You could

hear everyone walking around above you, and I'm sure the first floor could hear us stomping around in our literal combat boots. The cooks worked some strange hours. Oftentimes, they would come in at 3:00 am, all drunk, and proceed to shout, sing Beatles songs, and just generally play grab ass for an hour or so. Then they would jump into the showers, where all this noise continued. It would be 5:30 am before things quieted down to the level where we could get back to sleep. We had to muster — no, that's not something you put on a hot dog. It means "showing up for work," in a big military way. You didn't want to miss muster — trust me.

This noisy-cook business really started to bother all of the guys on my floor. We sent a group down to talk to them a few times. They would say, "Yes, yes, yes" and then just do it again that night. Even the brass didn't want to mess with the cooks for fear that they would masturbate in their chowder or something. Cooks in the Navy are a real *prima donna* group.

Another thing about the Navy is the posting of watches. We would guard our barracks 24/7. Someone would be walking around, making sure there wasn't any funny business going on. The worst watch was the "Dead Man's Watch," midnight to 4:00 am. You would "pull" a watch. Every few weeks, I would pull the Dead Man's Watch. Walking around with a flashlight and checking doorknobs and *Playboy Magazine* collections.

My daytime job at the old Philadelphia Naval Shipyard was in the sail lockers. Naturally, there wasn't a big call for sails back then, but we were there if *The USS Constitution* called and needed a few spinnakers or mizzen heads. An old Chief Petty Officer ran the sail locker. Being a Chief "Petty" Officer doesn't mean he would nitpick all day. It was a designation of rank — E6, to be exact. Though, for all intents and purposes, the guy treated me quite well, and we got along just fine.

One day, I was parked on an old desk in the sail locker, having a cup of Joe with my boss, and the subject came up about the cooks going all drunk-ass crazy every night. He'd been wondering why I'd been nodding off during our conversations about important sailcloth matters. So I filled him in on the dastardly deeds that were being perpetrated upon my person by the culinary staff.

So, on this particular day, the old chief said to me, "Goodman, if you go in the back, you will find a big wad of fiberglass insulation.

Take a handful of that and rub their beds down real good. Then, make sure you re-make the beds when you're done, so they won't suspect anything."

Well, that's what I did. I was on Dead Man's Watch that night, so it was easy for me to walk down to their floor and enter the bivouac. No one would question me, because it was my job. I went down there and rubbed all their beds down with the fiberglass insulation and then re-made the beds.

Sure enough, that night, they came in drunk, grab-assing and shouting numerous obscenities. Finally, they went into the showers, where all of this racket continued. Finally, they turned in.

About a half-hour later, we heard a bunch of cursing. They were screaming bloody murder down there. Then we heard the showers come on full-bore, and they seemed to be in there until about noon the next day.

After that, we all slept the entire night through. There wasn't a peep from the cookies downstairs. If any of them raised their voice, you could hear people "shushing" them — *"Shhhhh! Don't wake those guys up, whatever you do!"*

Mainiac Chowder

*M*aine is not a place to go if you're interested in getting a tan — or maintaining your sanity. They call them "Mainiacs" for a reason.

Years back, I spent a season up there in blueblood heaven. I went up there and restored an old "Cape"-style house located right on the Saint George River. It was in a little town called Warren, Maine.

The river was tidal, as most of them are up there. Naturally, this Old Salt went up there and figured out the tides using sheer willpower and intuition alone.

It didn't work.

I bought an aluminum "Bass" Boat and a small outboard motor. It was a 3-horsepower Evinrude and barely pushed the boat with my fat ass in it.

One day, I was downriver, messing around and waited a touch too long in returning to my berth. Traveling back upriver, it was taking everything that little engine had to offer just to fight the tidal river that was forming. It should have been an indication to me, but, then again, I'd been in the Navy, so nobody was going to teach me anything about saltwater tides.

Well, I must have been asleep when the Navy was offering the course on "Tides," because, when I finally got to my house, it was a shock for me to see my dock located about 60 feet away from the nearest water. That was mighty peculiar, because when I'd left on my little sortie, I simply walked out onto my dock and stepped right into the boat from it.

Needless to say, I had to get out of my boat. When I did, I immediately sank up to my knees in the most foul-smelling mud you have ever tasted. It was downright horrible.

Using a short length of rope, I sloshed my way up to my dock with a maximum of effort.

The next day, I drove down to Thomaston and bought a tide-chart table.

Soon thereafter, I was downtown on a sunny day — which, I came to find out, was as rare in Maine as a group of Democrats. I visited the local fish market. There, on a shelf, were these huge pieces of Cod. I could not believe the size of these things. Plus, they were cheap. I looked around because I was convinced that the guy in the flannel shirt had made a mistake in pricing these things. (*Everyone* in Maine wears a flannel shirt.) So I bought a pile of this "Salted Cod."

The thought occurred to me that I should go out and get all of the ingredients for a real New England fish chowder. (You have to say that last word correctly. It is pronounced *"cha-dah."* In fact, it helps if your nose is listing 30 degrees to starboard when you say it.)

I went to the farmers market up on the main road and bought fresh everything: potatoes, celery, onions, garlic, and a copious amount of half & half to fill it all in.

Then I proceeded to chop and dice, parboil, and assemble this culinary delight. By the time I was finished, the pot on the stove was about the same size as one of those garden buckets you put weeds in when you're refreshing your tree lawn.

One major thing about chowder is that it has to simmer. I want to find the guy or girl who invented the simmering process. Do you realize how much propane gas that requires? To simmer a large — OK, *extra large* — pot of fish chowder all day? That's exactly what I had to do. This stuff had to be done to perfection.

Finally, after about as much time as it takes to start a new civilization, the *cha-dah* seemed to be done. It had simmered all day, and I decided that I was going to sample it as soon as the propane-gas guy left.

With great anticipation, I procured the perfect spoon and dipped it into my bucket of white miracle soup. Slowly, I brought it up to my lips, and then — well, my lips puckered so bad that I couldn't get them separated for about 20 minutes.

That entire pot of *cha-dah* became chum in the Saint George River.

A few days later, one of the only Mainiacs who would even speak to me — he had a very pronounced nasal northeast accent — stopped by to BS with me. So, I told him about my cha-dah episode and the PTSD I was experiencing ever since it had occurred.

He looked at me with a questioning look on his face and then slowly said, "Did you soak the Cod?"

I said, "'Soak the Cod'? What are you yammering on about? No, I did not soak the damned Cod."

Well, as it turns out, you have to soak Salted Cod until you retire from a government job before you can use it for anything.

Whoever heard of soaking a fish in water? That's ridiculous!

House Party

*R*ecently, my wife and I were streaming on our little Roku player and found a movie called *AWOL*.

It was an interesting little piece that dealt with a few women who had alternative lifestyles of a sexual nature.

That, in itself, wasn't at issue. What caught our attention was the fact was that the movie's action was purported to have taken place in our hometown — two towns, to be exact: Plymouth and Noxen, Pennsylvania.

I went to school in Plymouth. I spent 12 years there and whiled away part of my youth at Oldfield's Pool Hall. My buddies would duck over there at lunchtime to buy cigarettes at three cents apiece from old Mrs. Oldfield. Then, we'd rack up a game of 8-Ball, and they would smoke their brains out.

But that's not the point of this story. This involves the town of Noxen, Pennsylvania.

Noxen isn't actually a town, per se. It's more of an area. There isn't a Main Street, an old courthouse, or anything like that. There is — or, I should say, there *was* — an infamous barroom called "Torchie's." This bar was the type of place that was a fistfight waiting to happen. It wasn't my type of place, but it did serve the inhabitants of Noxen. Those inhabitants, the scuttlebutt on the street had it, all stemmed from only one or two families in the town. There were lots of rumors involving fathers and their daughters. Now, all this was conjecture, but when you hear something about a place over and over, and it's always the same news with the same details, it is hard to simply dismiss it out of hand.

Anyway, one day Louie and I were out smoking hashish and riding around in my 1956 Thunderbird. It had two cherry-bomb mufflers on it and a big V8 engine. We used to ride the country road listening to that exhaust note, up and down hills in second gear, just out getting high and stupid.

Well, on this particular day, we needed a drink of something, so we popped into Torchie's Bar in Noxen. Both of us were sporting long hair, because it was back in the early 1970s, when that was the fashion in most of the

Western World, except, of course, in Noxen,
Pennsylvania. We were just sitting at the bar,
all gooned up on good hashish and sipping a
beer, when I realized that the locals were not
too pleased with our appearance — or our very
existence, for that matter — and had decided to
alter reality a little. This meant that Louie and I
would probably never be seen again, not if the
boys from Noxen had their way.

So we escaped. That's one benefit of having a
large V8 under the hood: They come in handy
when you have to run away from a bunch of
daughter-rapers and the occasional screaming
chain saw.

But that, also, is not necessarily what this story
is really about, either.

The main point of this story centers around
the area of Noxen *in winter.*

If you knew who to ask, you could rent an old
country house in Noxen rather cheaply. Usually,
they didn't have running water because the
pipes would be frozen. But these rentals were
not for long-term living purposes, anyway. A
bunch of guys would rent these houses just to
throw wild parties. In Pennsylvania, the legal
drinking age was 21 at that time. I wouldn't be
surprised if it is *still* 21 today, being that there
are "Blue Laws" in that commonwealth.

So having a place that would allow the beer and booze to pour freely was an advantage. That is where the house in Noxen came into its own. They were usually those old-fashioned, two-story affairs, set back from the main roads. Most of them were old farmsteads that had been deserted or inherited along the way, but the end result was always the same: Drinking parties.

At one of these parties, I asked where the bathroom was. They pointed and said to just walk through that door. As it turned out, there was a drop of about 20 feet into a pile of urine-soaked snow. Someone had ripped off the old porch that should have been there and left this crazy hole in the universe. Over the course of the evening, more than one drunken reveler stepped out into oblivion when they passed through the "bathroom" door.

Because there wasn't any water, a few of the longer-term residents went without a shower or a bath for several days — or for at least as long as the booze held out. A couple of guys would stay in the house over the weekend. One of them called the local nursing school and invited all of these frustrated nursing students out to this glamorous party.

As soon as an acquaintance of mine, "Ducky,"

heard this, he decided it was time to smarten up a bit to improve his chances of getting lucky. I watched him as he sprayed copious amounts of "Right Guard" deodorant under his arms — with the shirt still on, I might add. Then he doused himself with "Brut" aftershave to add that masculine touch that was sure to attract the opposite sex.

Whether or not the budding relationship was ever consummated, I'll never know. I left that house party just a few minutes before the State Police raided the joint for underage drinking.

I often wonder whether any of the arresting officers would need to use the bathroom at any time.

Mister Lucky

*O*ne day, my wife said to me, "Does every Goodman have to soup up everything that has a gasoline engine?"

Naturally, my answer was simple: "Yes."

My brothers and I grew up mired in oil and grease. We were the "Sons" in "William Goodman & Sons Excavating and Trucking Company." Consequently, any function we ever performed for my Dad's enterprise had an engine attached to it somewhere.

I started out when I was about eight years old, checking out our trucks for the next day. This entailed climbing underneath them and popping the plug out of the rear-end differential to check the oil level. Then I moved on to the tires. Air pressure was important when you had eight tires on a vehicle. Under the hood came the oil, power-steering fluid, and radiator. I was then required to sweep the dirt out of the cab and, at least once a week, clean the windows and mirrors. This was all part of the basic maintenance that went into operating a trucking business. Having ties to the Mafia was also a prerequisite, but we won't go into that right now.

Besides preparing the trucks for their daily grind, I also served as a helper on a coal truck. That, I have covered in other stories about being a coalman in Northeastern Pennsylvania, where all of the anthracite coal used to come from. I say *used to* because of the greed that ruined the industry, which was rendered a death blow when they dug under the river and flooded all the underground tunnels where this coal came from. It was called The Knox Mine Disaster; it happened in 1959 — you can Google it. There are some pretty powerful images of tossing entire freight-train cars into this giant hole in the riverbed — a feeble attempt to stem the flow of water that went on for days and days. They called these huge train cars "Gondolas," and they were used to transport coal in. Hundreds of them went into that hole in the earth.

But I'm digressing from my original intent here.

Being that everything we did had an engine attached to it, I started driving at an early age.

I remember my grandfather teaching me how to drive in his old World War Two Jeep. It was the real thing. It even had a star painted on the hood. We would go blueberry picking up in the mountains around Dushore, Pennsylvania, and, when we reached the dirt roads, he would let me drive. But you had to be careful. If you didn't shift the transmission correctly, it would jam between gears, and he would have to take the top off to un-jam it. That would be the last of your driving lessons for the day.

When we went blueberry picking, it was work. Sure — it sounds romantic: "Blueberry pickin' with ol' granddad." But unfortunately, that wasn't the case. He would have 6 to 8 of those 12-quart galvanized-metal buckets in the back of the Jeep, and we had to fill every one of them. It was hot, sweaty work, crawling around in the blueberry patch picking these little berries, three or four at a time, all day — from early in the morning until just before dark.

Again, I have wandered off the point of this story, haven't I?

Being that everything had an engine, racing these things would be a logical pursuit, and that is what I did. I raced cars.

I went out on the back road behind our house and bought a 1952 Ford from Mr. Steele.

He was one of the farmers who lived on the mountain where I grew up. I think I paid $35 for this thing — a 4-door Ford Fairlane with a flathead 8-cylinder engine.

I raced at the Plymouth Flats, a dirt oval track where they just bulldozed an oval into the topsoil. "The Flats" was an area near the Susquehannah River. Every year, it would flood during the winter months and deposit fresh topsoil. I think they called this an "alluvial plain," similar to that found at the confluence of the Tigris and Euphrates Rivers, where Adam and Eve screwed up our inheritance.

They had an old, crapped-out water truck that would make a few passes between each heat, but it didn't matter. After the first loop around that track by 20-odd automobiles, the place would be transformed into a dust bowl. You literally couldn't see your hand in front of your face. The thing to do was get behind another car and just roar away until you smashed into something.

The first thing I did was to gut the interior of my car. Everything that could even *possibly* burn had to be removed. This included the seats. We'd find one of those fiberglass kitchen chairs, one whose seat was contoured, and bolt that to the floor. Then, we looked around the junkyard for any 1957 Ford car. They had the original seatbelts in them. In 1956, Ford had decided to put padded dashboards into their cars, and, by 1957, most were equipped with seatbelts. A lot of people don't realize this. No one would use the seatbelts, and, so, a few years later, Ford stopped installing them. This helped us, because there were some basic safety rules at The Flats, and having seatbelts was one of them.

The next thing was a ¼ keg beer barrel. This was used for the gas tank. It was mounted in the trunk area and could hold only a few gallons of gasoline, which was the whole point. It was a matter of lightening the weight of the car and providing a modicum of safety. We would remove the bumpers and anything else that wasn't welded to the car. There wasn't a lot of protection in these things when we got done modifying them.

Last, but not least, was the custom paint job. Some guys would paint flames down the side of the car, but the way I looked at it, with the right hit from another car, there would be real flames to contend with.

I painted the side of the car with four aces, one from each suit in the deck — clubs, hearts, diamonds, and spades. I called my car "Mister

Lucky." In big letters, right above the splayed-
out aces, were the words, "Mr. Lucky." My
mother went ballistic when she saw that. It
was bad enough that her 14-year-old boy was
racing in a stock-car race — let alone having
"Mr. Lucky" emblazoned on the side of the car.
Oh — I almost forgot. There were also plenty of
"STP" stickers all over the car, too.

I chopped off the exhaust system and left just
a few feet of pipe right from the engine, and I
picked up a set of two deuces for the engine.
These were carburetors — there were two of
them, and each had two barrels. Hence the
name "two deuces."

My ride was set. NASCAR, here I come.

The fateful day arrived, and I brought "Mr.
Lucky" down to the track. The other drivers
were duly impressed with the paint job and the
engine sporting two carburetors. I was a force
to be reckoned with on that dusty day.

The entire object of the sport was to roll your
car over. That earned you a badge of courage.
Maybe a little stream of blood running down
your face — not too much; just enough for
effect. That, along with the brown dust, would
announce that you were the Alley Oop of the
racing world. You were The Man — 100%
Beefsteak. Of course, when you consider that a

race would last no longer than a minute or so, you could be called a "100% Beef Minute Steak Man."

Well, I raced that day and made it around the track a number of times. I never won anything, nor did I roll the car over, so I had just the brown dirt on my face *sans* the blood line. I'd failed to use deodorant that morning, and I didn't attract the sweet young car groupies I had expected to, but it was all a learning experience.

I ended up selling "Mr. Lucky" to a guy for $50. He made it just once around the track before the engine just exploded. I guess all the gasoline from those two deuces was a bit too much for the old engine. I left the area in a hurry with his $50 tucked away in my blue jeans and said goodbye to "Mr. Lucky."

Big Shot Contractor

*T*hrough inheritance, I ended up owning a mobile home, set on a concrete foundation, located in northeastern Pennsylvania.

I rented to the same guy, Stanley, for more than 13 years. One day, my wife and I were driving past, and I casually said to her, "Do you see that house right there? Well, someday, I will come back here and build you a dream home."

Needless to say, I never thought that she would hold me to my promise. Years later, after he father passed on, she decided that we should move back to Wilkes-Barre. At the time, I had a very lucrative advertising business going on in Charleston, South Carolina, and was not the least bit interested in giving that up to move back to Death Valley.

But women have very persuasive ways when it comes to nesting instincts, and I ended up capitulating, selling the business and moving back to that shithole. Braced with the profit from the business sale, I proceeded to build her dream home. I started in1996 and kept at it for four years, non-stop construction.

The first thing that I did was to excavate the foundation completely. The place had a water-drainage problem because it had been built on a solid granite ledge and didn't have any sort of French drain system to wick the moisture away. While I was digging up the entire area, I decided to replace the septic system and install all new pipes into and out of the house. This is accomplished by using what is commonly referred to as "PVC," plastic piping.

One day, I was down in the bottom of a seven-foot hole next to the rear of the building, installing a new two-inch PVC pipe that was to service the kitchen sink. I had an old wooden ladder in the hole with me to help with the prospect of getting in and out of this hole in the ground.

Teresa was standing at the top, looking down at me with casual interest while I worked in the dirt. From her vantage point, I had the shoulders of an elephant and the head of a pea. That's what it looks like when you're staring straight down at someone — their head is much smaller in proportion to their body.

It wasn't the easiest task fitting these pipes

together — they came out of the foundation at a weird angle. So, I had to twist and turn the various elbows to get the right pitch of the thing so that the water would flow downhill, a rather troublesome consideration when you are dealing with drainage pipes.

Finally, after expending my entire U.S. Navy choice vocabulary of four-letter words, I managed to glue everything together and was ready to climb out of this miserable grave.

It was just then that Teresa said, "Excuse me, Jason. But did you want that pipe to go through the ladder like that?"

When I turned around and looked, sure enough. There was the fruit of my frustrating labors — a nice, new shiny plastic pipe that went from the foundation, through the rungs of the ladder, and into the wall of soil.

I told her to hand me my circular saw and proceeded to cut my 8-foot wooden ladder into two equal lengths. I also told her that if she ever mentioned this to anyone ever again, I would do something nasty to her that involved dirt, holes in the ground, and a lack of oxygen.

Driving Like Mr. Bond

*A*ustralia has always fascinated me.
I remember reading everything that I could get my hands on as a kid about this country "down under." In Vietnam, I had quite a few dealings with guys from Australia. They were there fighting just like I was, and we would invariably meet in one of the establishments along Tudo Street, a main drag in Saigon, aka Ho Chi Minh City.

In 1970, right after I returned from Vietnam, I bought a ticket on a tramp steamer and was supposed to sail this tub to Australia. But I met my first wife and cashed in the ticket — less a 10% charge — and bought a Triumph motorcycle.

My next chance came in 1976, when I answered an advertisement looking for teachers to go live and teach in Australia — and I just happened to be an art teacher at the time. I was awarded a contract and found myself living in

Melbourne for a few years.

I soon became acclimated to a teaching and living routine after being there for several months. I met a few people and ended up with two decent friends. One was David, who worked for Foster's Brewery, and the other was Neville, who worked for Tobin Brothers Funeral Directors. There are a few stories about this period in my life in the first book in this series, *Urban Gothic.*

David was a member of the Returned Servicemen's League. This was an Australian organization somewhat like the U.S.'s Veterans of Foreign Wars or American Legion. The Returned Servicemen's League honored the fallen comrades at the battle of Gallipoli with an elaborate ceremony that they performed every Sunday night at sundown. Another thing the RSL were noted for were their snooker tables. David was a really good snooker player, and I showed promise because of my ill-spent youth hanging around pool halls back home in Plymouth, Pennsylvania.

As a snooker team, David and I would make a handsome pile of cash when we played at the RSL on Sundays. The Australians didn't have a term that was the equivalent of "dirty pool," but that's what snooker was all about — dirty pool. You could be losing a game by hundreds of points but, through a number of nefarious moves, end up winning the game.

One Sunday, we decided to take a drive down the coast on The Queen's Highway. It ran along the coast of Victoria and made its way all the way over to Adelaide in South Australia. We were headed toward a little beach town named Apollo Bay.

So, we started our journey by playing snooker in every town that had an RSL hall. By the time we hit The Queen's Highway proper, we both had a tidy sum of loot in our pockets from sharking poor bastards out of their hard-earned money. David would allow me to break and then step in when the time was right to run the points up and win the game. Every snooker parlor had these wooden beads on wires above the table. You would use the tip of the cue stick to slide the tokens over as the game progressed.

Well, finally, we hit the Highway — built, obviously, either by or in honor of the Queen of England at some time or another. We had money and a case of Melbourne Bitters in the back seat of my Volkswagen Beetle.

There I was, flying along this two-lane twisty road. I was up and down, shifting, pumping the brakes, and literally flying around corners.

During the entire ride, I had a can of beer between my legs. David and I were just rolling along, having a high time of it. We were both pretty well greased by this time, and the fact that we'd paid for our entire vacation with our snooker money just made the whole thing sweeter.

Well, we pulled into Apollo Bay just in time for a nice seafood dinner. Isn't youth great? A little food and a shower, and Boom! We were ready for more. There was a nice club with a bar not far from our hotel, and the girls were all out that night. It didn't hurt that we were high rollers, either, with our snooker loot burning a hole in our collective pockets.

Well, all good things must come to an end. After two nights of pillage and debauchery, we were flat broke again, and it was time to move on. Plus, our little holiday was over. It was back to work the next day, so we decided to drive back the same way we had come.

This is where the situation presented itself.

We used The Queen's Highway again on the way back. It turns out that the road actually hugs huge cliffs above the pounding ocean. Some of these cliffs were easily 800 feet high in places, and the real kicker was that there weren't any guardrails at all!

As I drove, the thought of winging blindly around these curves a few nights prior made me sick to my stomach. I had no idea this road was as dangerous as it was.

I finally asked David, "Hey, David. Did you know that this road had these sheer drop-offs all along its route?"

He told me that he did.

I said, "David, did it ever occur to you to tell me about these deadly drop-offs?"

He said, "Why? I thought you knew about this road, and I guessed that that's why you were driving like James Bond all the way down here."

Bahama Nights

My first wife's mother started the first coupon-clipper magazine in the United States. It was called *The Yankee Trader,* and the thing was a runaway success. Within a few years, it was making millions.

Sometimes, they would trade things for advertising in this publication. So, one day, her mother came to us and asked, "Would you like to take a Windjammer Cruise?" Naturally, we both said, "Yes!"

The Windjammer Cruise was exactly that: You picked up the ship in Nassau and then sailed to the out islands — also known as cays — in the Bahamas. Our ship was their flagship at the time. It was called the *Phantom* and had been built by Ari Onassis as a gift for the Princess of Monaco. How the Windjammer Cruise acquired this vessel is beyond me, but she was a beauty. (I use the past tense here for reasons I will explain shortly.)

The *Phantom* was a steel-hulled, four-masted schooner. It was a really beautiful boat. This craft could accommodate 90 guests, spread out in 45 cabins. Their *modus operandi* was simple: They sailed at night. You could put your name on a list and helm the thing. I used to be a helmsman in the U.S. Navy, so I jumped at the chance to steer this ship with all of that sail above my head — an exhilarating experience, to say the least.

One night, when we were all gathered around the bar onboard, the skipper asked if anyone wanted to get married. He was a bona fide Sea Captain and could legally marry people on his ship. So, in a haze of rum-induced fever, my girl and I stood up there with three other couples and were married aboard the *Phantom* somewhere in the Caribbean.

Years later, I was in Florida and just happened to be reading the *Miami Herald* when I ran across a story of tragedy. *The Phantom* had been lost at sea off the country of Belize, trying to outrun a hurricane. The skipper — the same one who had married us — went down with his ship, along with 16 other crew members. So one might say that my first marriage was definitely annulled by Neptune and that the paperwork now rested in Davy Jones's Locker.

But that isn't what this story is about.

We spent a week aboard the *Phantom* enjoying this Windjammer Cruise. The ship would anchor off these small islands and transport the guests onto the beach with a motor launch. They would set up a bar-b-que on the beach, and we would while away the hours eating and swimming or just exploring the island, looking for buried treasure. Then, around 5:00 pm, they would pull up anchor, run up a ton of canvas, and we would be on our way, just sailing around, looking for another island.

One night the mate told me that, later that evening, we would be sailing across the very tip of the Bermuda Triangle. He went on to say that this was the only time he'd ever get a little nervous on these cruises. I didn't think much of it until later.

My new wife and I had one of our tremendous arguments. She wasn't feeling too well — sea sickness. She was plain miserable. So, I decided to take my frustrations out on the liquor supply in the bar.

During this entire cruise, we got to meet several of the other guests, and some were more friendly than others, considering the tight quarters of a classic schooner. One couple were from Bulgaria. They were quite charming, but the only thing that really stood out was their height. Both of these people were more than six feet tall. The husband was at least 6 feet 9 inches and his wife another 6 feet 7 inches.

I was having a good time telling the bartender all about my theories on women and why they were bad luck on a sailing ship. We were yucking it up until the wee hours of the morning. I did my best to liberate the contents of a bottle of good Cuban rum and nearly succeeded. The boat was that much lighter the following morning.

At 1:30 am, the bartender announced that he would be closing the bar, so I stocked up on my last drink of the evening and had him put it into a Bimini walking cup. Then I proceeded to the forward deck. I knew that I would be in a heap of trouble if I came busting into the cabin with half a load on, so I decided to get some clean ocean air prior to facing the music that my newly minted wife would be playing on my behalf.

It was beautiful. I was standing on the deck, overlooking the ocean. Above me, four masts of sail was flapping in the breeze like only that much canvas can do. The air was the perfect balmy temperature. It was one of those nights that you could enjoy forever, if you understand my meaning.

Just as the earlier conversation with the mate started to replay in my mind — the fact that we were in the Bermuda Triangle and all that goose-bumpy stuff — I happened to look to my left.

Do you remember those early depictions of death? You know — the ones where a skeleton is wearing this long, black, silky gown, with the big hood and the flowing sleeves. Do you remember that?

Well, when I glanced to my left, there it was: Death was walking up the rail, in my direction. The moonlight was shining off the silky fabric. This being, this apparition, was at least 7 feet tall and was slowly making its way along the rail, directly toward me!

My fingernails started to bite into the wood of the railing, my hair was standing on end, and my knees were knocking together. *Death* was coming to take me away!

Just as I contemplated jumping over the side, this phantom of the night approached and, in a deep Bulgarian-accented voice, said, *"Gooood eeeefning, Jaaaasoooon."*

It was the voice of Count Dracula — the pronunciation was every horror movie that I'd ever seen. The words reverberated around me like cold, fleshless fingers, grasping at my sanity.

And it all culminated in the realization that this was the wife from the couple that we'd made new friends with — from that nether region, that country of blood-sucking demons, Bulgaria!

My first order of business when I returned to my cabin was to rinse out my blue jeans, which had, somehow, acquired a yellowish stain on the front of them.

Condo Living

*M*y first wife's mother was a millionaire. That, in itself, doesn't sound too impressive today, when everyone talks in terms of billions. But, back in the early '70s, it meant a lot to me. I didn't have that kind of money.

Well, her mother bought this one-bedroom condominium in South Palm Beach, Florida. Actually, South Palm Beach was originally called Lakeworth, Florida. But the condo builders felt that it would add to their bottom line if their cheesy structures would have an address with such a — how do you say it? — *pedigree* attached to it.

We moved down there after my wife flunked out of college in Wilkes-Barre. Wilkes-Barre, Pennsylvania, is such a despicable place that I'm surprised that anyone who flunks out of college there doesn't commit suicide.

So her mom found this university, gave them a substantial donation, and they said they would

take her in and, eventually, gave her a degree.
Don't get me wrong. My first wife wasn't stupid.
Far from it. Her intellect was far superior to
mine. She was a very smart young lady at that
time. Her trouble was depression. She hated
where she was going to college, and I didn't
blame her. Wilkes-Barre was a disgusting place.

  Back to South Florida.

  We both enrolled at Florida Atlantic
University, and everything seemed to be just
peachy. I found a little job and made enough
money to get by. That means putting gas in my
car and buying cigarettes. She, of course, didn't
have these issues, meaning a lack of money. But
understand something: Rich people don't give
money away to their daughters' boyfriends.
That just never happens — in case you were
licking your chops at the prospect of getting
rich by fucking a chick whose parents have a
few bucks in the bank. I have seen it before —
you won't get squat. So, I didn't get squat, and I
didn't ask for squat, either. I earned my money
the old-fashioned way — I worked.

  But when you live in Florida, a nice perk is
having a beach at your disposal after work —
or even before work, if that makes you happy.
Maybe the surf is up — no problem: Just grab
your board and hang ten.

One of the interesting things about this condo complex in South Florida was the fact that Charles Atlas lived there. You probably don't remember Charles Atlas. He was a body builder way back in the '50s and '60s. His body would appear on the back of most magazines that young guys would bother reading. And, man, was he pumped up! This guy was ripped! He said it was all due to his patented technique that he called "Isometrics." It had to do with tension on the muscles and other stuff that has no bearing on this story, so I'll just say, "Google it if you're interested."

Mr. Atlas didn't socialize. He actually hated people and just wanted to be left alone with his little girlfriend. Please keep in mind that this was in 1972, and, by then, Charles Atlas was probably 80 years old, but he still looked good.

Next to our condominium complex was a big golf course, so all of that beach was available. One day, I was up there snorkeling when I spied Charles with his girlfriend. She was short and fat. She looked like a 55-gallon oil drum with little stick legs. As I watched from my submerged place, he bent over and extended his right bicep to his girl. She grabbed the big muscle with both hands; he lifted her off the blanket, and they both went for a dip.

This was significant at the time. I spent some of the '50s and most of the '60s trying to emulate Mr. Atlas. I wanted desperately to look like him, with all of those giant muscles bulging out. Man — I could've gotten any girl had I looked like that. That same perception wasn't lost on Charles Atlas, and that's why he owned a condo in South Palm Beach, Florida.

One night, I was standing on the walk, smoking a cigarette and just contemplating how broke I was, when I spied a twin-engine plane doing strange things. It was three o'clock in the morning, and this airplane should not have been flying up and down the beach like it was.

I knew a little about the subject. My brother owned his own plane, and he would take me flying whenever I was home. He would explain everything about the plane — taking off, landing, and, especially, about putting the thing down at airports. There is an established pattern to the way planes land. They don't just barrel in and drop on the ground. They have to execute all these turns and line up with the runway. All the while, the pilot is talking to the control tower, who is telling them what is going on in the air around them.

This plane wasn't doing any of that. It was just flying up and down the coast, just a half mile offshore.

The next day, it was on the news. The plane was carrying bales of marijuana — tons of the stuff. They were supposed to land at Palm Beach International Airport but were tipped off that the cops were down there waiting for them. So, they jettisoned their cargo and flew away. Twelve bales of high-grade pot washed up on the beach at the golf course — the one I used to snorkel at offshore. It was all wrapped up and didn't even get wet. Millions of dollars worth of pot, and I just stood there, watching this plane fly up and down, up and down, and, all the while, I was worrying about where my next tank of gasoline was coming from.

Hell — I could've bought the whole gas station.

The Shadow of a Smile

*R*ichard was the husband of my mother's best friend, Catherine. Mary T. and Catherine grew up together in Newark, New Jersey, and remained dear friends for 78 of their respective 86 years of life.

Richard and Catherine lived in Irvington, New Jersey, and would come to visit us at least once a year. We lived on the side of a mountain in Pennsylvania. We were poor. Richard was not. He worked for The Boy Scouts of America. He was a real bigwig in that organization, traveling the world and becoming a vice president in due time.

My memories of Richard are these: he always had a nice automobile, usually a fairly new model. Also, he dressed to the nines. Richard always looked good, his clothes impeccable, sharp creases in the shirtsleeves — "dapper" would be the right word with which to describe Richard's overall appearance.

We were pretty poor. The road up the
mountain to our house was dirt at that time
and fraught with danger. It would wash
out whenever we had a heavy rain, and the
Republicans would take forever to come and
fix it. We had chickens, an outhouse, a pump
well, and all of the other trappings of a family
living in poverty.

But that didn't matter to Richard and
Catherine. They would pick a fine Sunday,
jump into their nice car, and drive up to
the wilds of Pennsylvania for a visit, usually
staying the entire day. It really made Mary T.
happy when they'd come to see us.

As time went on, my father, "The Big Duke,"
somehow got in with the Mafia, and we
became rich. We had so much money that
my mother, Mary T., became a Republican.
The Democrats eventually got into office and
paved the mountain road up to our house, and
Richard's car no longer got all dirty when they
came to visit.

The interstate was finished between
Pennsylvania and New Jersey, much to the
chagrin of The Big Duke. So we started
driving down to Irvington to see Richard and
Catherine at their house. The old route would
take forever to get there from where we lived,

mostly secondary roads, with a lot of messing around with lower speed and bad surfaces. But the new road fixed all of that.

As the years went by, we all grew older, which, for some reason, seems to happen to everyone I
know. Anyway, Richard got sick and was dying in the hospital in Irvington, New Jersey. My mother asked me to drive her down there, a request that I could not refuse under any circumstance, and so I did.

When we got to Richard's room, there were Catherine and Richard. He was lying in the bed with some tubes going into his arms, and, much more importantly, he was in a coma. The nurse said that he hadn't moved — or anything — for at least four days. He was just lying there, as if sleeping.

But the troublesome thing that I noticed was his five-day shadow. Richard had the start of a beard. I'd never seen him with any facial hair for my entire life. He was always well dressed and equally well groomed. It was more than a little disconcerting.

I sat there for a while, looking at Richard and getting more and more annoyed at his appearance. This wasn't right. Richard should not look this way, especially in a coma.

Finally, I got up and left the room. I went to every nurses' station on those few floors, putting together all the equipment I would need to execute a clean shave. I found a brand-new disposable razor, a stainless-steel basin, towels, and some nice shaving cream. But the *tour de force* was the aftershave. I stumbled onto the remains of a bottle of English Leather.

I proceeded to shave Richard. First, I got a wet towel and wrapped his face in it. Then, I applied the shaving cream with exaggerated movements and flourishes — and then started with the razor. I started talking, making up stories to tell him, just like any of my barber friends would do, telling tall tales that ended when you paid the guy. Finally, after a complete shave and a nice wipe-down, I applied the aftershave — a very liberal amount, I might add, just for effect.

As I was cleaning up the area, putting everything into the stainless-steel basin, I turned and looked at Richard. On his face was a small, almost indistinguishable smile. Even Mary T. and Catherine noticed it.

Richard was happy.

The next day, he died, but he was a clean-shaven man when Death came for him, and I know Richard would have appreciated looking his best for that final occasion.

A Crushing Event

*W*hile under contract to the Education Department for the state of Victoria, Australia, I was assigned to a "Technical School" in a town called Dandenong.

In Australia, a "Technical School" was, basically, where all the working-class children were sent. The upper classes went to what was called an "Academic School." The biggest difference between the two kinds of schools was the emphasis on "Shop" classes at the Technical School. They offered considerably more Shop classes than an Academic School did.

One of my responsibilities at that school — a responsibility I found out about rather abruptly one day — was that I had to teach two hours per week of PE, Physical Exercise.

And I hated every stinking minute of it. Standing out there in the middle of a grassy field watching some punk kids kick a ball around was not my idea of a good time. But it was explained to me, in no uncertain terms, that this was compulsory. Period.

So, there I was every Tuesday afternoon, standing there, feeling my feet slowly going numb from the wet and cold grass in that miserable field.

One day, Salvation came knocking on my door.

For some reason, I had to go across campus to the "Shop" section. This wasn't a place that I was familiar with, because I was an Art Instructor, and I wasn't allowed to be seen with "Shop" types.

I'm kidding, of course — but not by much.

So, there I was, next to the woodshop, when I realized that there was too much building for the size of the shop that I could see. I asked the teacher, a person who used to come by my apartment with his latest conquest that his wife didn't know about. At least, I don't think she did. I asked him what was on the other side of the wall, and he told me that it was an old, unused weightlifting gym. He said they'd put it in years ago but could not find anyone to teach the subject. So, they just locked the place up and walked away. At least until that fateful day when Jason came along.

Through a series of steps and missteps, I went

to the school administrator and got permission to use this little gym. Also, I asked if this might count in fulfilling my compulsory PE teaching requirement. And, it did.

I put together a team of 21 14- and 15-year-old students of mine and used Charles Atlas as an example. I promised them huge, bulging biceps and triceps, perfect for those good-looking "Sheilas" who showed up on the beach when the warm season came around.

We went in there and started to clean the place up — it was covered in dust. But as the room unfolded, I realized that, whoever had put this thing together knew exactly what they were doing. There were several sets of free weights and bars and a complete rack of dumbbells — every possible thing you could wish for when you flexed your muscles in the bathroom mirror. Speaking of which, there was even a complete shower room — with lockers. The place had been perfectly built for my needs. I envisioned myself there, with nice warm, dry feet for the duration of my contract at the school.

Well, I offered this as an alternative to kicking a stupid ball around and got a good response. I had to actually turn people away. The place appealed to that mysterious longing for huge biceps and triceps.

One day, we were in there, lifting heavy pig iron, when one of the class fuck-ups — you know: every class has its clown — was particularly annoying.

Australia has its own set of anti-discrimination rules, just like we do, covering the usual areas of race, religion, and creed. But somewhere in the small print is a clause that deals with class fuck-ups — the proverbial "class clown," "dunce," "cut-up." Call him whatever you wish. They are the same anywhere in the world.

You must realize that all of this happened in slow motion — the ol' "Slo-Mo" that they talk about at sports events. I turned around after this class fuck-up shouted something really absurd and watched in absolute horror as he began to careen backwards. That wouldn't have been bad in itself. The problem was that he was holding this bar with a bunch of weights on each end. They looked like cast-iron wagon wheels.

There he was, holding the bar just under his chin as he proceeded to slowly fall backwards.

The potential conclusion to this event flashed through my mind: This kid, lying on the floor with his brains squirting out like a bag of lumpy gravy. A huge *Squiisshh!* Followed by the impact of the iron on the wooden floor.

I saw myself being run out of the country by a band of people with angry faces, with things flying at my head, down at the docks. The headline would read, "Iron Clad Murderer Ousted from the Fatherland," or "Brain Matter Merchant Thrown Out of Australia."

Then came the sound of the weights impacting the floor. I had my eyes closed by then, not wanting to witness all of that gore flying across the room and getting on my shoes.

But the gods of Charles Atlas were with us that day.

The bar landed right under the kid's chin. He had enough weight on it that it barely cleared his throat and windpipe.

Naturally, I went nuts on this startled and completely shaken class fuck-up, although, secretly, I was interested in seeing the crushed skull and brain matter dripping off the nearest wall.

The things you see when you don't have a camera!

Hot Rod Testis

*M*y wife once said, "You Goodman guys would soup up a lawnmower if you had one."

Her observation was absolutely correct. My bothers and I were all big on drag racing when we were young. Every one of us had a hot car. What that means is an automobile that has been altered to produce the maximum amount of horsepower that an engine could take and still function.

I remember one such car. It was a 1934 Plymouth — one of those Eliot Ness-type cars from the Roaring '30s. We installed a huge 8-cylinder engine that had come out of an old Lincoln. It was known as a "Flat Head." The reason for that designation was its design.

Without getting too technical, allow me to explain that a modern engine has its intake and exhaust valve system in the "head," whereas a "Flat Head" engine has them in the engine block. Hence the name "Flat Head," because the cylinder heads were just that — flat.

We souped this thing up by installing Eldenbrock aluminum cylinder heads, which increased the compression ratio. We also installed 4 2-barrel carburetors, also known as "four deuces." This was a lot of carburetors for *any* engine — let alone a Flathead 8-cylinder.

This thing was fast. We ran it at the drag strip as an "H Gasser." It's difficult to explain what this means in simple terms. "H Gas" was a designation that the Hot Rod Association used. It was based on a formula of weight-to-power ratio and a lot of other impressive-sounding terminology. But, rest assured: "H Gas" did mean that this car was hot. It could do "Stop" to 60 mph in about 10 seconds. That may not sound impressive by today's standards, but trust me — it was impressive as hell back in the 1960s.

People don't realize how small the front seat of a 1934 Plymouth was. By comparison with modern standards, they were very narrow. Two adults seated in the front seat would have their shoulders pressing together. For this reason, we had to place the gas pedal all the way over on the right side of the cabin. The clutch and the brake pedals were in the same place as any other car, and the three-speed shifter was between your legs.

To augment the gas pedal, we installed what was called a "Moon" gas pedal. The name was a trademark of the company that made them. They were shaped like a large cartoon foot and were chromed to beat the band.

This is where one might encounter a problem.

Every Sunday, we would take the car on a trailer to the Pocono Drag Lodge, the closest certified drag strip to where we lived in Pennsylvania. We would drag race for money and, occasionally, a little trophy. For those who don't drag race, allow me to explain.

Quite simply, a drag race is a straight line, one-quarter mile in length. You would sit there, at a dead stop, revving your engine. Then, when the flag dropped, you popped the clutch. The front wheels would come off the ground , and the car would go like a bullet — hopefully, in a straight line — for the quarter-mile. Whoever reached the finish line first was the winner.

At this time, allow me to explain why the entire lineage of the Goodman line was altered by drag racing. As I explained earlier, the cabin of a 1934 Plymouth was extremely small — gas pedal way to the right, shifter between your legs. In the heat of battle, with the engine roaring and the finish line a faint haze on the horizon, your competitor was right next to you, trying to get his front fender past yours. There was heat blowing up from the engine, the smell of gasoline in your nostrils, and the roar of straight pipes under your feet. All the while, you're in the second gear of a three-speed transmission.

At this critical time, you'd look at the tachometer and decide that it was time to shift into third gear. So, you'd grab the white knob of the shifter, and, as soon as the tach told you to do it, you'd smash the gear-shift knob back into third gear. At that point, this white knob, attached to a chrome rod, comes flying back at great speed — right into your balls.

And it hurts. In fact, it hurts quite a bit.

Our only consolation for having won this drag race may have been a $100 bill and a small, chrome-plated trophy.

The fact that you could never have children was just collateral damage.

You won the race — and that's all that mattered back in 1964.

Talking Trash

*F*or a number of years, I lived in a little beachside community called "Briney Breezes." Actually, my place was in Boynton Beach, Florida, and the area known as "Briney Breezes" was a trailer park on the ocean. I kid you not.

It was the only one left. The area was all established mobile homes and double-wides with its own beachfront. It was a strange lot who lived there, but we won't go into that right now, because it sets a course way off of our heading.

In Boynton Beach, at least out there on the beach, the people were very particular about their trash. If you put out the wrong items, in the morning, the trash guys would just leave them there for you to deal with.

So, one day, I was standing at the Gulf gas station, right across the entrance to "Briney Breezes." I was telling my buddy — the guy who ran the place — about all my trash woes. An old man was sitting there, nursing a bottle of Miller High Life, and he must have overheard our conversation.

Suddenly, he piped up, "You know what yer doin' wrong, don'tcha?"

I replied, "No. I don't think I'm doing anything wrong."

He said, "No, no, no. I'm talkin' about yer trash problems."

I said, "OK — I'll take your bait. I'll bite. What am I doing wrong with my trash?"

He proceeded to give an entire 15-minute educational dissertation about trash and its disposal. Finally, he seemed to be getting to his point.

"Them Black boys is sensitive to their calling in life. Sometimes, they feel disrespected because they're just trashmen. Well, young fella, here's what you have to do. Go to the likker store and buys you a pint of "Wolfschmidt" gin. It's gotta be that brand, and I'll tell you why the next time we meet. Right now, I gotta go."

Well, I did what he told me. Went up and bought a pint bottle of the gin he'd suggested. Then I placed that bottle right on top of the trash pile in my can so that they couldn't miss it.

Lo and behold, the next morning, everything

was gone, and the trash cans were placed neatly by my house, not just tossed into the alley like they used to do. From that time on, I could put just about anything into the trash, and it would disappear. I mean radioactive waste products like an engine block from a 1959 Chevy BelAir. You name it —I put it out there on Wednesday night, and *Voila!* Thursday morning, it was history.

Weeks passed, and finally the day arrived when I roared into the "Glup" station on my big Yamaha motorcycle — that's what we called it: "Glup" rather than "Gulf." There he was — the same old man, just sitting there in the shade, drinking a cold bottle of Miller High Life Beer — the one that always came in a clear bottle. I went up to him and asked him if he wanted another beer, and he said, "No. I only drink one, 'cause I'm walkin' home."

I told him about how well the little hint that he'd given me concerning the trash had worked. I mentioned the dead bodies, the radioactive waste from the nuclear power plant that my boss told me to get rid of — and everything else. He just sat there and smiled.

Finally, after listening to my bullshit for a few minutes, he said, "Do ya know why I's told ya to put out only Wolfschmidt gin? "

Naturally, I had no idea, and I told him that.

"Well, ya see, when them Black boys get high on that there gin, the very next day, they's can drink a quart of plain ol' water and get a good buzz all over again for nothin'."

Truck Driver

I spent a number of years in south Florida. Most of my university work was done down there, at Florida Atlantic University in Boca Raton. But because of my allergy to snow and the temperatures in Pennsylvania during the winter season, I usually hung around down there until the weather cleared.

During those episodes of blue sky and perpetual sunshine, I found myself in the position of having to make a living. For this, I fell back on my trucking and heavy-equipment skills that had been ingrained in me from an early age by my dead Dad. Usually, I worked as a bulldozer operator, which is an interesting concept that I must tell you about.

Normally, when I worked in that capacity, the company would provide me with a relatively new Mack Truck, with a nice "Low Boy" trailer. Sitting on top of that trailer was a brand-new Caterpillar D-6 bulldozer. A D-6 can fill the average-sized living room — they are big machines, and they occupy a lot of space.

The blade on the front is 12 feet wide. Think about that. A normal traffic lane on the Interstate is exactly 12 feet wide, so my blade went from the shoulder line all the way out to the white lines, and I could see nothing behind me while tooling down I-95 in south Florida. On top of all this, they would pay me about $7 an hour! I never understood that. Here they were, giving me responsibility over a half-million dollars worth of machinery, and then they'd skimp on my wages.

An old man once told me that half of your pay in Florida is the sunshine. Over the years, I found out that he was absolutely correct.

One time I showed up for a job "interview" for operating a large bulldozer. The guy was a real redneck, and we immediately got off on the wrong foot. During the conversation, he asked me, "Boy, can you grade within an inch with that there machine?"

I responded, "Yes, sir — I can. But not for $7 an hour!"

Without going into too much technical detail, let me just say that grading level ground over any considerable distance with a big bulldozer and getting it to within an inch — well, consider how difficult that task really is. Go ahead. Hold up your fingers and make an inch. You have to have the "eye" to do that — and, I must say, I did. With all ego aside, I was pretty damned good with a bulldozer. But working all day under those conditions is quite stressful, to say the least.

Anyway, I worked for this company named Shaw Trucking, out of Fort Lauderdale but with a yard up north in Delray Beach, close to where I lived. They were a decent outfit to work for, and I got along well with the bosses and other employees.

But when there wasn't any work for the 'dozer, they would send me out as a truck driver. One day, when I complained to the boss man about driving a truck, he said, "Look at it this way: You're the highest-paid truck driver in the entire company!"

When they sent you out in the morning, the boss would say, "Just go out there, take Number 64, and show up at the pit." Now, "Number 64" was a big truck. It was all checked out and fueled up, and the keys were in the ignition. But no one ever bothered to tell you anything about the truck. You had to figure it out on your own — how to start the engine, where all the different gears were, what kind of brakes it had. Just about everything that went into driving that truck was up to you to decipher.

At times, this could be a bit trying. For example, my old man never had any automatic-transmission trucks, so, consequently, I didn't know squat about driving a truck with an automatic transmission. They are, of course, quite different from trucks with a normal stick shift. But, in a very short period of time, you had to figure it all out and work that truck for the next eight hours, driving from Point A to Point B with a huge load of dirt in the back.

So, one day, they sent me out as a truck driver. We were supposed to haul this dirt to a housing estate and fill a hole in the ground. That was the day I was sent out in "Number 64."

Every big truck — every dump truck, that is — has a unit on it called a PTO, aka "Power Takeoff." This unit transfers power from the transmission to an hydraulic oil pump that fills the cylinder that dumps the load of dirt. Some have levers sticking up out of the floor — two levers: one to engage the PTO, and the other to release the oil pressure, which allows the big box of the truck to lower. Most trucks have the two levers, but there is another system that uses a large red button that you pull out to engage the PTO, and then there is another little switch that lowers the truck "body," as it is called.

We were delivering this dirt to an established neighborhood. It was one of the older ones in south Florida where they still had the overhead wires going across the street. So, I wheel in with my load of dirt, back up, and pull the red button to dump the material on the ground. I pulled out, pushed the other button to let the box come down, wheeled out of the site, and proceeded to roar down the street.

Everyone was waving to me and shouting, so I waved back, shouted some obscenities back at them, and continued on my merry way.

Unbeknownst to me, I had failed to really disengage the PTO, and so, as I drove down the street, the back went up again, into the air, and proceeded to tear down every wire that crossed over that street.

I didn't realize what was happening until I stopped at the intersection at the end of the street. All of the phone lines and cable TV wires were lying on the ground for the entire length of the street. My coworkers had been waving and shouting, trying to get my attention, and I'd ignored them.

Well, needless to say, it was a very long time before they asked me to be a truck driver again. When there wasn't any work for the bulldozer, they just sent me home and got someone else to drive "Number 64."

The Great Tire Massacre

*T*his story might be an apology for a stupid thing that I did years ago in Key West, Florida. I have no idea if anyone is listening or if anyone actually cares, but I'll tell the tale anyway.

Allow me to lay the groundwork for the story. It was back in the mid-1980s that Teresa and I lived in Key West. I can honestly say that this wasn't one of the better periods in my life. I was drinking a lot and doing stupid stuff.

Earlier in the year, I had been injured — rather severely — in an industrial accident. So, when I applied for a job with Clarence Keevan & Son, they asked me to write a disclaimer for the accident that I'd had with one of their competitors, Toppino, Inc.

Both of these companies were trucking and excavating firms, my good ol' standby when it came to drunken debauchery-type of employment situations. You know the kind —

practically mindless jobs that allowed a person
to drink heavily and still get by. It wasn't like
I was drunk on the job, but let's just say that
my powers of observation and deduction were
somewhat limited on The Day After — in some
places, this is called "The Irish Flu."

Clarence Keevan had a number of vehicles,
but the one that plays host to this story was
his aluminum dump trailer. I know that you've
seen these in your travels but probably have
never thought much about what they were
used for. A "dump trailer" is just that — a
trailer that dumps. I'm not trying to be farcical
or disingenuous here — I tried to look up the
word on my LanguageMaster, and "…a trailer
that dumps…" is the best that I could do.

Anyway, the "dump" part of the trailer is
very large. It's made from aluminum, so it's
very light. They are used primarily in Florida,
because there's so much sand down there. You
don't see too many up north, because the rocks
and dirt would tear them to pieces. I would
wager that you never thought dump trucks
could be so specialized.

This type of trailer is hooked up to a truck
called a "tractor" — which makes no sense,
because it's obviously a truck. But, then, one is
already hard pressed to define the term "tractor

trailer." In essence, that's what it means: A truck/tractor hooked up to a trailer equals a "tractor trailer."

This was used to transport materials, although the few times that I drove the thing, I hauled materials to the landfill up on Boca Chica Key. One day, my boss told me to run that load up to Boca Chica, so I jumped up on the side of the truck and looked at the load. It was about 40 tons of asbestos water pipe that they'd dug out of the Navy base on Stock Island. When I saw the load, I almost flipped. This stuff was highly classified material, a huge pollutant, with cancer-causing agents and sheer death for anyone who came within 50 feet of the stuff. I'm exaggerating, of course, but it still presented certain "issues," you might say.

I drove the load up to Boca Chica and pulled up on the scale. The guy in the scale house asked me what I had onboard, and I told him that it was a lot of old pipe from the Navy base. I wasn't going to tell him the whole truth. Hell — this stuff was supposed to be double-bagged in black-plastic garbage bags with a lot of red tape. Back then, "asbestos" was a household word that spelled doom and disease for everyone.

But, for some reason, the guy got suspicious

and decided to go look at the load for himself. Nothing I could say would dissuade him. When he climbed up the side of the dump trailer, he almost went nuts. He started screaming about it being asbestos and immediately started to blow his nose all over my truck.

Then he told me, "You pull over there and give us your keys! We are impounding the truck — and you, as the driver — until this is sorted out!"

He definitely impounded me. For more than eight hours, I sat there. My boss was furious because he needed that truck and trailer for another job. I was nothing more than a footnote that morning.

Well, phone calls went back and forth. I think someone, somewhere, at some point, called Washington, DC, and spoke to the Pentagon until finally the scale guys were told in no uncertain terms to allow me to dump this load. I went out back and asked the bulldozer operator where he wanted this load of 40 tons of toxic waste dumped. He pointed and said, "Over there. I'll just push some dirt over it."

And that was that.

All of that fuss and mess, and nothing really came of it besides a 10-hour day for me.

But I should get back to the relevance of the

title of this story.

That dump trailer had a reputation. I don't mean that it put out or anything like that. But it did carry around a stigma for having sticky brakes. Every trailer of that nature usually has a set of "Maxi-Brakes" on it. These are a safety feature that automatically applies all of the brakes if you lose air pressure (compressed air is what operates the brakes on most trucks). If you fall below a certain pressure, like 60 pounds, the brakes will kick on and will not release until the pressure is above that threshold.

Well, one day, Mr. Keevan asked me to take a load of stuff up to his private island. It was called "Shark Key," and it was *his island.* When things were slow at work, he would send us up there to work on developing it for million-dollar housing sites. We built roads and installed underground pipes, etc. — all the trappings of a millionaire-to-be's paradise.

It was the end of the day. I was tired and pissed off. I didn't need to be told to drag this load of crap up there at six o'clock in the evening. But, he was the boss, as they say.

I rolled up and dropped the load, which is to say, raised the aluminum body and "dumped" the load on the ground.

That's when the trouble started. The Maxi-Brakes wouldn't disengage.

I tried everything I knew to release those brakes, but to no avail.

For some reason, I couldn't simply disconnect the trailer and just leave it there, and I couldn't call into the shop because the two-way radio was on the blink. There was plenty of air pressure. Those things were just *stuck.*

Then I tried an old technique — called "breaking" the wheels. You put the truck into low gear and just drag the trailer for a short distance, to try to "break" the wheels free. You alternate going forwards and backwards.

So that's what I did — back and forth, back and forth. Then beads of sweat started to form on my forehead; they started dripping off the end of my nose. I was getting angry. I called the truck every dirty name I could think of.

That's when I made a stupid decision. I gunned the engine and started dragging the entire sonofabitch toward the main gate — all 1.5 miles of the distance.

Earlier that day, the mechanics had installed eight brand-new tires on the dump trailer. This was a big deal, because Mr. Keevan didn't spend large money easily. Most of his stuff was kind of jury-rigged together, if you catch my drift. So, for old Clarence to spend a couple of grand on new bananas for his dump trailer was quite an offering.

Well, guess what happened.

As I was dragging Mr. Keevan's dump trailer with its brand-new set of eight rubber truck tires at $400 apiece, something happened.

Over the roar of the diesel engine, I heard an explosion. It sounded like a cannon going off. Then there was another, and another — until I counted a total of eight explosions. Every single one of those brand-new tires were scraped flat on one side until it hit the place where the air is kept — and *Kablooie!*

I parked the truck and hitchhiked home.

Puerto Vallarta Grocery

*T*hroughout the mid-2000s — wait: that just doesn't sound right. I mean, you can say, "the mid-1960s," "the mid-1970s," and you could go as far as to say, "the mid-1980s" and "the mid-1990s" — but "the mid-00s"? Here in Ireland, they sometimes call zeros "aughts," so, could we have "the mid-double-aughts"?

Anyway, Teresa and I were spending a considerable amount of time in Mexico — Puerto Vallarta, to be exact. It was a great town, and the temperature never fluctuated more than 10 degrees — 75 at night and 85 in the daytime. When you consider that, in Pennsylvania, where it was a balmy 6° above zero, Fahrenheit, living in Mexico just made more sense.

The small hotel we used was located on Aldama Street, just three blocks from the *malecon* (Spanish for "jetty." We would call it "the place where lovers stroll along the seawall.") It had 10 rooms — that was it, 10 — and one of those was used as a laundry room. So, technically, there were only nine rental units.

These "rooms" were more like small one-bedroom apartments. There was a kitchen, a living room, and, due to some Mexican law, a separate bedroom. The law said you had to have a "substantial" wall separating the sleeping area from the communal living areas.

Because I always booked Room #10, we also had the added benefit of a spiral staircase in the living room that went up to a private sun deck on the roof.

But that wasn't all. In the bedroom were two large louvered doors that opened onto a small private balcony with a spectacular view of the bay.

You may have noticed that I haven't mentioned the name of this hotel, and I have no intention of doing that — and for a good reason. After Jose died, everything changed. Jose was the manager of this little "boutique" hotel. He was a beautiful, gay Mexican man. Every year, I would siphon money to him in $500 increments until I'd paid the $3000 for a three-month rental — January, February, and March, every year for a solid several years.

Jose told me that he used that money to keep the little hotel up and running all summer, their traditionally slow time of year. My money paid salaries and made basic improvements on the place, like fixing the hot water in our bathroom. We went for three years without hot water in our shower — which, if you know Mexico at all, is one of those *mañana* type of things, *señor.*

The last year we went to Puerto Vallarta, Jose called and apologized for not being in the position to pick us up from the airport. He said he was in Guadalajara, in the hospital. I asked if it was anything serious, and he assured me that it was practically routine. I spoke with Jose only one more time before he died of cancer that had attacked his sinuses.

That's why I won't tell you the name of the place.

On a slightly happier occasion, Jose was entrenched in his meticulously kept apartment just off the interior kidney-shaped swimming pool, just past the lobby.

Because we had a kitchen, many nights during our stay, we would prepare small, simple dinners for two, served on the balcony overlooking Banderas Bay, complete with candlelight and nice, soft music.

Because of this, one or both of us would have

to make a trip up the road to a *supermercado* —
a supermarket. Oh, there were small Mom and
Pop stores sprinkled all over our neighborhood,
but their prices would often fluctuate — exactly
proportionate to our fluency in Spanish, and
their selection was somewhat limited. It was
definitely *not* the place to go to get soy sauce —
trust me.

One afternoon, I decided to take the plunge
and go out to the store. So, I walked the three
blocks to the northbound bus lane and jumped
on "The Rattler." We called the local buses
"Rattlers" for a very sound reason: They rattled!

These buses were something of an institution
in Puerto Vallarta. No air conditioning, plenty
of pictures of The BVM and Christos over the
driver's head, and many, many grinding-gear
shifts. Not to mention the fact that everything
around you was rattling.

Guys with guitars would get on and stand
down front, belt out a tear-jerker Mexican *canto*
about the *señorita* who got away, and then walk
down the aisle with their hat, collecting a few
pesos from the bus riders. I mean, you could
listen for free, but what kind of image would
that project? A tightwad, typical cheapskate
American *gringo,* for sure. Hell, when the peso
is trading at 16 to the dollar, a 5-*peso* coin isn't

going to break the budget, and, if it does, you have absolutely no business being in freakin' Mexico anyway! So, pay up, pal, and enjoy the culture.

Whew! It's pretty high up there on my soapbox — and to think I suffer from vertigo.

Anyway, there I was, rattling my way up to the *supermercado,* going for some basic Mexican groceries.

I used the same store quite a bit, so I could nod at various employees upon eye contact as I made my way up and down the various aisles, picking up items, including a few extras to nourish my vicious sweet tooth.

At the checkout, I carefully packed away every item into my nifty "Greenpeace" or "World Koala Bear Fund" canvas bag with two sets of handles, the long and the short.

Forty-eight dollars later, I strolled out of the store, very conscious of the "Pinot Grigio" sticking up from the center of the pile of neatly packed groceries. I walked out to the highway and boarded a southbound "Rattler" for the trip downtown.

As we approached my stop, I moved toward the back-exit steps and stood in the stairwell so I could see the streets flying by. Oh, yes — I failed to mention that the Puerto Vallarta bus drivers go like hell, and they like to drag-race one another in the process.

When my stop came up, the door opened with a *Hiiisss!* of compressed air. I set my bag on the last step while I navigated my disabled legs onto the street — and then it happened.

The bus roared off, leaving me standing in a cloud of noxious diesel fumes while listening to the doors slam shut with pressurized air.

My groceries, my yuppie *"I Was Stupid Enough to Donate Hard Cash for a Species I Could Give a Rat's Ass About"* canvas bag — with the two sets of handles, one long and one short — went roaring off with the "Rattler." But, much more importantly, I lost my "Hey, Mon" laid-back persona and started shouting really dirty words at no one in particular.

There I was, The Ugly American, red-faced, angry expression of all my years of a carefully groomed image of this really cool international dude who doesn't speak a word of Spanish, high or low.

My cover completely blown, I ran — well, walked very fast — up to the northbound street and waited for every bus.

As they arrived, I would jump into the doorway and say, *"Por favor"* a few times and attempt to describe my $48 bag of groceries.

Now that I sit here writing this down, I realize how completely deluded and naïve I really was. Did I honestly think that this nice, juicy bag of beautiful groceries, complete right down to a good bottle of Pinot Grigio wine — did I really think that it would be sitting there, behind the bus driver's seat?

"Señor Goodman, si — a few very good Samaritans have entrusted me, Juan, the bus driver, with your precious little canvas bag of groceries with the image of an orca whale silk-screened on the front."

Finally, I realized that this was the ideal definition of the idea of "Exercise in Futility" and gave up. I had leapt in and out of at least a dozen hot, noisy buses in a vainglorious attempt at altering an entire, well-established culture.

With my resignation came the realization that I had to save face. I simply could not go home and face myself, let alone my wife, with the fact that I had allowed my groceries to become lost in the hard, cold reality of culture clash at its finest.

The acceptance wasn't sitting well on my palate. I couldn't very well blame some mustachioed *bandito* with a thick accent for liberating my white, American groceries.

I hailed a taxi and rode back to the same *supermercado,* re-purchased the exact same $48 order of groceries, right down to the same vintage Pinot Grigio, and proceeded to leave the store. As I approached the automatic door, the manager, who I knew from numerous head nods, stopped me and asked me the ultimate question.

After 10 minutes of pure lament, a sterling performance that would not leave a dry eye in the house, at the very summit of my "Poor Me" range, he said,

"*Señor*, you have made someone extremely happy!"

I left with my brand-new canvas bag full of groceries, the one with a very cute Mexican donkey silk-screened on it, a donkey that had an uncanny resemblance to someone I knew.

I had made someone not very happy, but *extremely* happy!

Yum, Rhubarb Pie

*M*y mother-in-law couldn't cook worth a damn.

She was your basic meat-and-potatoes person. But if you knew my father-in-law, you would understand why.

John liked things pretty basic. One time, I went out and bought all the ingredients for a real Irish-style dinner — I was going to surprise John. Everything was fresh — cabbage, potatoes, and a nice piece of corned beef. At the time, I assumed that was typical Irish fare — corned beef and cabbage.

Since I have started living in Ireland, however, I have come to see the error of my ways. (In Pittston, Pennsylvania, corned beef and cabbage was an Irish dinner, so that's settled.)

Anyway, I spent the better part of a day preparing this feast for my Irish-American father-in-law. When five o'clock rolled around — John's typical suppertime — I presented him with the fruits of my labor.

Unfortunately, he was not impressed. He just picked at a little cabbage and ate a small potato. That was it.

Afterwards, when the kitchen was all cleaned up and we were settled in the middle room, John turned to me and said,

"Jason, I want you to know that I really appreciated what you did today, but if the truth be told, I've never cared for corned beef and cabbage."

Then he returned to despising Ronald Reagan, who was appearing on the television set at the time.

I mean, Ann, my mother-in-law, had a couple of special dishes that she prepared — Yorkshire Pudding comes to mind. But she stuck to the simple stuff — no fancy vittles for her and John.

What Ann lacked in cooking, she made up for with her mastery of the oven. Man, that woman could bake! She really did a number on pie crust. She made the best pies I have ever tasted.

Unfortunately, that's where the problem began.

Shortly after I met my wife, Teresa, after we went through the various rituals of dating with a possible future in mind, I was, of course, invited to her parents' house for dinner. Now, the dinner was your basic meal, and I will say that it was nutritionally sound. The food would keep a human being alive, but there wouldn't be any memory of it afterwards.

Let's put it into context. Teresa had told me in advance what to expect, and I was definitely looking forward to a nice, freshly baked pie emerging from her oven soon after the sacrifice of dinner was completed. I wasn't to be disappointed.

Or so I thought.

When Ann placed a nice pie in the center of the table, the entire kitchen filled with the smell of this freshly baked treat. It is my understanding that you can tolerate just about anything for dinner, provided it is followed by a really good dessert.

As Ann started to cut the pie, she said, "Jason, I baked this pie special — just for you. I heard that it was your favorite."

Naturally, I was quite impressed and humbled by this thoughtful gesture. I immediately began to speculate as to her source of information and glanced lovingly at Teresa. With pure affection in my eyes, I blinked when Ann said, "It's your favorite, Jason — a nice rhubarb pie!"

The reality struck me like a hot kiss on the end of a cold fist.

Rhubarb pie?

I fucking *hate* rhubarb pie!

Naturally, I was thinking all of this when I turned to look at that vile stuff. With a sickening smile, I told Ann how grateful I was and actually said, "Yum, yum!" quite a bit.

She placed this steaming pile of dog turd in front of me, and I choked back the bile that had begun to rise in my throat. My next statement was a question:

"Do you have any ice cream?"

After spooning almost a half-gallon of vanilla ice cream all over that piece of pie, I proceeded to shovel the stuff into my mouth, chomping and repeating, "My, my — rhubarb pie!" over and over again, all the while thinking of the delicious pain I was going to inflict on the person who'd provided this despicable piece of propaganda.

For more than 18 years, I've traveled with my wife, Teresa. We've lived all over the United States, spent months down in Mexico, and enjoyed the sights on Malta and Singapore. We traveled completely around the world on one occasion, spending months in exotic places. But we always return home — usually for the holidays — and every time I set foot in that house on Cole Street in Pittston, Pennsylvania, there was the smell of a freshly baked pie.

Yes, sir! You guessed it! A big, perfect, double-crust *rhubarb* pie!

Dry Clean Only

*I*n the year 1976, I was awarded a contract to write curriculum and teach in Australia.

My posting was a "Technical School" in a suburb of Melbourne. For part of the time of the couple of years I lived there, I leased an old house in a small town called "Upwey."

This place was like an old whore who wears entirely too much makeup. It had seen its heyday in the 1930s as a place where the rich and famous would go to in the dead of summer, when the temperature stayed in the 90s day and night. Upwey was located in the Dandenong Mountains, which actually had snow on them for a good part of the year.

The one important article of clothing I packed was an old, beat-up fisherman's knit sweater. It was sort of a good-luck charm.

One cold morning, I wore my old friend to work because our classrooms were cold —

especially in the early part of the day. I looked more like a homeless man than a well-paid educator, but being "…an artist…" allowed me some leeway in the apparel department, and I took full advantage of that eccentricity.

While teaching a girls' class, one of my 14-year-old students started to admire my fisherman's knit sweater. She went on to say that her mother could knit me an identical copy of my sweater. You might say I was receiving an offer to have my fisherman's knit sweater "cloned"!

So, considering that my left shoulder was currently exposed, due to the failure of my Frankenstein stitch job, she had my undivided attention. That afternoon, when the temperature mimicked my impression of the "Outback" region, I stripped off my sweater and gave it to the student.

A few weeks later, the little 14-year-old came by the Teachers Lounge and left a rather bulky package for me. When I got home, I opened it and found two sweaters — my original DNA host and a brand-new, almost-identical copy. But when I put the thing on, it dropped to my knees. This brand-new copy of my old, trusted fisherman's knit was more than a foot too long!

Still, it was replete with all of the intricate

cable-knit accents and garnish. Now, I can't claim to know a thing about darning or knitting needles. I know they click a little when you use them and that old biddies made copious pairs of bulky socks with them, but, for all intents and purposes, that is where my library of knitting information ended. However, as ignorant as I was, I did know that to knit an entire extra foot of an elaborate sweater is not an easy task. Finally, I decided that this mother was popping "Black Beauties," and I was trying to figure out how to get a handful from her — discreetly.

I returned the sweater with a note explaining that, unless I experienced a rapid-growth event, this sweater was not wearable.

In time, it came back to me, all finished and of the correct length. It even had the heavily woven waistband at the bottom.

My colleagues, after closely scrutinizing the sweater, informed me that the initial knitting was labor intensive, but for the woman to have to undo it was even harder. Myself, I couldn't say one way or the other.

About a month later, the school had a parent/teacher night, and I met my student's mother. After a stream of apologies, this woman said, "Mr. Goodman, I'm sorry for the mistake. You see, I 'got into' the beer one night and kind of lost all sense of time."

I thought to myself, *Hell, I want a few cases of whatever you were drinking, lady.*

Shortly thereafter, I commissioned two more fisherman's knit sweaters, one of which she made using choice "Merino" wool. They were absolutely spectacular.

Finally, my contract ended, and I returned to the United States, but, prior to leaving, I built a large wooden crate and packed it full of a few years of memorabilia. There was a case of Foster's Lager, aged Tawny Port from South Australia, aboriginal musical instruments, and my three brand-new fisherman's knit sweaters.

It took months for that crate to arrive at the Mafia-controlled docks in Newark, New Jersey. I had to go to the World Trade Center — the original — twice, just to get the proper paperwork for them to release my crate. Then, I made two trips to the docks, and they could never find my stuff. Before my third attempt, I told a friend of Italian persuasion about my troubles, and he said, "Did you grease all the guys at the dock?"

So, on my third try, armed with a pocketful of $50 bills, they suddenly located my errant crate. These fellows couldn't do enough. They loaded the thing on my truck and even had the time to help me tie it down for the return journey. I was amazed at this transition.

After a few nights of hiking down Memory Lane, I grabbed my three fisherman's knit sweaters and proceeded to show them to Mary T, my mother. She was always saying, "Son, you have taste in your mouth when it comes to your wardrobe…." So, I wanted to put that fear to rest by showing her my handmade garments.

Well, about a week or so later, I went up to Mary T's house to collect my three choice possessions. As soon as I stepped into the house, I knew something was amiss. My feelings were verified when Mary T said, "Your sweaters smelled a little musty from being at sea in that wooden crate, so I washed them. Jason, you should have told me…."

I immediately thought, *Told you what? What is there to know about three beautiful, handmade fisherman's knit sweaters?*

It turned out that she had machine-washed and dried my three sweaters.

When I saw them, I started to weep uncontrollably.

There they were: Three tiny fisherman's knit sweaters, reduced to a child's size — more like the size of an infant.

Over my shoulder, as the salty tears rolled down my face, I heard my mother say, "I thought they were a synthetic material."

The Electric Bass Guitar

I have always wanted to play bass guitar. For years, I used to watch the bass players, and I realized that they were cool. I would imagine all of these young female groupies tossing their underwear up onto the stage at my feet. There I am, kicking out all of those deep, spellbinding notes — *Thum! Thum! Thum!* — the audience going wild, screaming for more.

But it never happened.

Allow me to relate the story about how my stardom as an electric bass player was sidetracked — although "sabotaged" would be a better word — from the very beginning. I'm like Nero, the Roman emperor who offed himself while saying, "The world has lost an artist!"

I was about 12 or 13 years of age and decided that I wanted to play a guitar. Those were the days of The Brothers Four, Joan Baez, and others. Bob Dylan was just starting to play the clubs in New York. Folk Music was all the rage, and I wanted to be a part of it.

I got out my mother's Sears catalogue and looked at the "guitar" section. There it was: a Silvertone Spanish Classical Guitar for only $22. This was your basic six-string model, but it was a beauty: silver body with those little squiggle things rather than one big sound hole. So I saved up my money and sent away for this life-changer. The operative word here is "saved" — as in, "I saved my *own* money."

The instrument was delivered, and I decided to find an instructor, someone who could get me past the first chord of the song "House of the Risin' Sun." I went every week and took lessons. I procured a "Mel Bay" book on *How to Play Guitar,* and I was soon on my way to instant stage stardom.

One day as I was walking into my guitar class, I heard this terrific sound. It was the *Thum! Thum! Thum!* sound. As I entered, there was my guitar guru, blazing away on this guitar with four big, fat strings. So I asked the stupid question, "What is that?"

He went on to explain that it was an electric bass guitar. I was smitten, sold, and bowled over. I made up my mind that I would have an electric bass guitar within days.

The next day, I was again paging through my mother's Sears catalogue, and I found my dream guitar. I told both of my parents that I needed to get a different guitar.

The first question my Dad asked was, "What's wrong with the guitar you have?"

I replied, "Nothing. It's just not the right one. I have decided to become an electric bass guitar player."

My Dad said, "No, you are not. You, young man, are going to learn to play *that* guitar first! Then we'll talk about this other item."

My mother chimed in, "What do you want to do that for? You'll end up standing in some smoky bar with a cigarette stuck on the end of the guitar neck, playing blues, and hanging around with ne'er-do-wells."

The thought never occurred to me to ask how my mother knew about sticking a lit cigarette on the end of a guitar neck in some old blues bar. Afterwards, I gave that question some consideration, and she just smiled at me and didn't say one word.

Well, this set off a German Battle of the Wills. I insisted on having my way, and my Dad was not inclined to allow me to ruin my life by sticking lit cigarettes on the end of the neck of my bass guitar in some smelly blues joint.

The conversation wasn't going anywhere
that evening — or any other evening, for that
matter. My father would tolerate my whining
for only a short period of time before he
threatened to place his size-11 shoe on my
up-and-coming-bass-guitar-player ass. We had
reached a stalemate.

Well, it was my stalemate, not his. I pointed
out that I had used my own money for that
six-string guitar, but he just told me that
the conversation was over. He had spoken;
someone had chiseled his words into stone, and
that was the end of it. No electric bass guitar —
at least not during his lifetime.

I got all pissed off and said, "If I can't play a
bass guitar, then I'm not learning to play any
guitar — so, *there!*" I went on to say, "If that's
how both of you feel, then I will become an
accomplished artist and poet who ends up
writing books about the subject, so, *there!* Put
that in your pipe and smoke it! Or, stick that on
the end of your guitar neck and, and, and —
well, that's it!"

I took my Sears Silvertone Spanish Classical
guitar and stood it up on a window seat in
my parents' living room. No one ever touched
it. It just stood there for about 25 years, until
one day, the neck just snapped, and the guitar

disintegrated.

Fifty-two years passed, and there I was, living in a little town called Lititz, Pennsylvania. One day, I was driving up South Broad Street and had to mail a letter. There was a postal box right on the corner, next to the Dosie Dough Coffeeshop. Next to the coffeeshop, there was a music store. So I pulled into the space out front, jumped out of my car, and *Wham!* I was knocked flat on my butt by an image.

There it was — shiny, black, with a really neat name: *Ventura.* Go ahead — say the word a few times: *Ventura. Ventura Electric Bass Guitar.* It was propped up on its own stand, right in the front window.

I quickly posted my missive and ran into the music store. I asked the guy, "How much is that black, shiny electric bass guitar — the one called *Ventura*?"

Things just kind of escalated from there.

An electric guitar sounds like crap until you plug it into an amplifier. I needed one of those. Then came the stand on which to rest the guitar. I also needed a strap, because the guitar was pretty heavy. As it turned out, I bought the shiny, black *Ventura* bass guitar, a "Crate" amplifier, and a black strap with a little white peace sign on it. Then the guy talked me into a

"Snark" automatic tuning device that you clip onto the head, and it makes it so much easier to tune the instrument. I also bought the flexible "Pigtail" cord, so that I would look the part up there onstage with B.B. King or Eric Clapton — you know: a couple of my buddies I could just sit in with, nothing really special. I also picked up a book on how to play the thing and a music stand to hold the book up with. It was the entire outfit, the complete deal.

I asked the guy, "How much?" But, remember, I assured him, that this is going to be a cash sale — greenbacks, my man, filthy lucre. No governors around here today, if you catch my drift. Hey, by the way, can you stick a cigarette between those string ends — right there? Only if you smoke? Is that the answer?

"Two hundred and fifty bucks for the lot."

He didn't care one iota for my jive talk.

I gave him the money, and I loaded the stuff into my car.

On the way home, I thought, *52 years, and I finally own my own bass guitar.*

I lugged all the equipment up the steps into my house and set it up in the evening room. I plugged in the amp, installed the cord, and got out the little "Snark" automatic tuner. I was going to fire this bad boy up.

In Vietnam, I served with the US Navy, Riverine Force. We operated in the Mekong River. On at least six occasions, planes flew over my boat, spraying Agent Orange. The flyboys would come right across the river and not even bother to turn off the sprayers. It would really piss me off, because I had to go out there and clean the decks off of this shit.

Well, guess what? Yep, I developed at least four different medical conditions from exposure to that stuff. One of them is called "Peripheral Neuropathy." What that amounts to is a loss of strength in the hands, unprotected as they were most times. I have a few other problems: asthenic heart disease and skin issues among them.

But for the sake of this little tale, it's the neuropathy that really matters.

After setting up all the equipment, I turned on the amplifier and cranked it up to eight. Man, I was going to blow out my own windows. I placed my hand on the neck and tried to form a basic chord of sorts — and nothing happened.

The string was buzzing off the fret bar. I didn't have enough strength in my hands to press the strings down properly on the frets. My bass playing sounded like crap.

After all that time — 52 years — and I finally

have the electric bass guitar that I'd lusted after so long ago, and now I faced this wicked twist of irony. Maybe a different set of adjectives might explain it better — mostly the four-letter types.

Well, that was about three years ago. I'm sitting in one of those Swiss leather types — the number with the separate leg cushion. And right there to my left, on its own floor stand, is my shiny, black electric bass guitar. It's really nothing more than part of the furnishings, a pain in the ass for the girl who cleans my house.

My only consolation is cranking up the bass settings on my home stereo and on the one in my car — *Thum! Thum! Thum!*

The Fritz Effect

*P*eople don't realize how cold it can get in south Florida. Over the years, I have spent close to 18 years on the Gold Coast. Most of that time was in pursuit of a college degree from Florida Atlantic University, in Boca Raton.

While working toward my Master's degree at FAU, I had two immediate concerns. One was money, and the other was a place to live.

Both of these basic Maslow's Hierarchy needs were to be met in one fell swoop.

I met Louis R. at his shop in Boynton Beach. He was the owner of a foreign-car-repair establishment. At the time, I owned a rare 1970 MGB "Split Bumper" car. It had an electric drive system that actually worked. If you know anything about English cars, you have had experience — usually bad — with Lucas Electrical Systems. Let's just say that they failed quite often.

When it comes to Louis R., I can't give you

his last name, because the man ended up doing some serious time as a guest of the Florida Department of Corrections. I can assure you that Louis R. was not the kind of person who ended up as someone's bitch while incarcerated. In my autobiography, *a. PUZZLED EXISTENCE,* I went into some detail about Louis and his nefarious background, but that's another story. Please don't confuse Louis with my other friend "Louie." They are two entirely different — as in "polar opposite" — personae.

As it turned out, Louis was looking for an experienced mechanic, *and* he had a large four-bedroom rancher with an available room. So, you could say that I stepped into clover that day.

I was hired as an automobile mechanic who specialized in English sports cars, mainly MGBs and Jaguars. This job was custom made for a graduate student, because I could set my own hours. Louis paid me by the job. It was a fixed rate and relied on a standard car repair manual that specified how many hours any given repair was supposed to take. Some jobs I could do easily within the specified time period, and others would take a little longer, but the pay was decent.

As for the room, it was a nicely furnished

house in the suburbs, with plenty of space, a typical South Florida rancher from the '60s.

The only drawback was Louis's crazy girlfriend. At that time, Louis was living with this really young and really spoiled Jewish-American Princess. She had to be the center of attention at all times and did not appreciate being ignored for any length of time — something I tried desperately to accomplish.

This girl would pick a fight with Louis because he read a lot. Naturally, a person can't read a book and pay attention to the trauma of being a rich young lady at the same time. Louis would sit in the living room reading a book, and she would jump around him, screaming at the top of her lungs about something to do with her car. She was always smashing her sports cars. I kid you not: there was a line of totaled automobiles outside the shop, every one of which was hers. Someone once placed a sign out there that warned of the effects of driving while ingesting Quaaludes. That really sent her to the moon.

So Louis would just continue to read until she got fed up with his serene disposition and tear his glasses off. Then she'd crush them into bits, twisting and turning them until the lenses popped out. Afterwards, she would storm out of the house and roar down the street in her sports car *du jour*. Louis, who was completely acclimated to this behavior, would then go into the garage and pull another pair of reading glasses out of his secret stash and proceed to return to his novel, until the phone call came about the car wreck.

The name of his business just happened to be "Foreign Auto Repair Technicians," conveniently rendering the acronym "FART" — and Louis had done this on purpose. With that said, you can imagine what kind of work environment it turned out to be.

One really cold morning, Louis asked me for a ride to the shop. The man hated cars and driving. He would have someone else drive any chance that he got.

One interesting design concept of the early MGB car was the space immediately behind the two bucket seats. I owned several of these cars and had always used that space for small suitcases when I traveled. Under the rug back there were two inspection plates that concealed two six-volt batteries that supplied the electrical needs of the car.

Another little quirk of those early MGBs was the fact that they would roast you in the summer and freeze you to death in the winter. For some reasons, those cars never had an adequate heating system. You owned a car like that for the challenge of driving — not creature comforts.

One thing that I have failed to mention was the fact that Louis also owned a very large German Shepherd dog by the name of "Fritz." Besides bumming rides with everyone, Louis always made it clear that Fritz would be coming along for the ride as well. Louis rarely went anywhere without Fritz.

So, on this exceptionally cold morning in Boynton Beach, Louis asked me to drive him to the shop. This wasn't a problem because I was going in to work, anyway. He tilted the seat forward, and Fritz jumped into the space behind the bucket seats and curled up for the ride.

As we drove up US 1, freezing, with all of the windows tightly closed, a really bad stench wafted over us. I looked over at Louis, and he looked at me. Simultaneously, we both realized that it was Fritz who had dropped the bomb into our environment.

We immediately started to gag on this German gas attack. Words like "Eeeew! Eeeew! Pew!" came to mind. Gasping, coughing, and grabbing for the window cranks, Louis turned to me and said, "That was The Fritz Effect…"

What Is Blue?

*A*s part of my graduate work at Florida Atlantic University in Boca Raton, Florida, I had to do student teaching. This was an important part of my overall grade. If I remember the facts correctly, student teaching comprised 20 credits of my final Master's degree program. In a way, you can say that I lucked out. They just happened to have an opening for a student teacher at the university experimental school, which was located right there on campus.

There was an incident where I was caught skinny-dipping in their pool by the campus security force — and I wasn't alone at the time of the infraction. But that, of course, is another story entirely. I did manage to talk my way out of the crime because I had worked in the university student works program, and that worked in my favor. Other than a stern tongue lashing and a solemn oath on my part never to do it again, the incident was completely buried from the watchful eyes of my masters at the time.

Anyway, I worked in this school for an entire quarter semester, which consisted of 12 weeks. I was tasked with educating primary-school students in the art of sculpture, which was my specialty at the time. I had a number of classes involving 20 of these little tikes. Even though I have been married three times, I've never had any children. Some of that decision was due to my involvement in Vietnam, and some was pure selfishness on my part. But, over the years, I've had a number of frustrated housewives tell me that I didn't understand what it was like having a bunch of kids underfoot.

I never had the heart to tell them how difficult it is to "teach" 20 of those little monsters for an hour at a time. Trust me: It isn't easy, especially when you factor in that the average attention span of a seven- or eight-year-old is about 20 minutes. It can get pretty interesting at times trying to control a classroom full of kids. This chore becomes even more pronounced when the parents fail to teach their kids any discipline and then pack them off to school and expect their paid teachers to provide surrogate parenting.

But my soapbox is starting to get the better of me. I've always had an issue with vertigo.

There I was one day, teaching a painting class to a bunch of 10-year-old girls. I distributed the water-soluble paints and the heavy card stock, along with some cheap paintbrushes, and everyone was just as snug as a bug in a rug. The little girls were sloshing away with the paint, and I walked around the room giving little comments on their progress into the world of Picasso and Dali. Everything was cool until I walked up to this one little person and commented on her landscape.

One of the other instructors had mentioned to me that this particular student suffered from a rare optical disorder called ACHM, or *achromatopsia*. Being the young, arrogant, know-it-all fool that I was in those days, I listened but never asked what this word meant, let alone how to pronounce it. I came to find out on that particular day.

As I commented on this young lady's painting, I pointed and said, "Why don't you consider using a little blue in this area up here?"

She turned around, looked at me, and said, "What is 'blue'?"

This ocular disorder, a rare, genetic thing, allows the individual to see only in gradations of gray tonalities. In other words, she could see only in black-and-white, and I was being asked to explain the color blue.

As I stammered away, I realized that this was entirely above my pay grade: *What is blue?*

*Allow me to express my gratitude for
your company on this journey,*

Jason

27867700R00204

Made in the USA
Columbia, SC
04 October 2018